# Contents

# Acknowledgments

Many of us don't quite understand ghosts. In this book, I have told or retold these ghost stories from a fictional perspective, trying from my comfortable place in the twenty-first century to make sense of the past. Throughout the work, I have endeavored to be as true to historical fact as possible.

The editorial genius and encouragement of Betsy Johnston and Barbara Purchia made this work that much easier. The photography of my husband, D. Peter Lund, was a great asset.

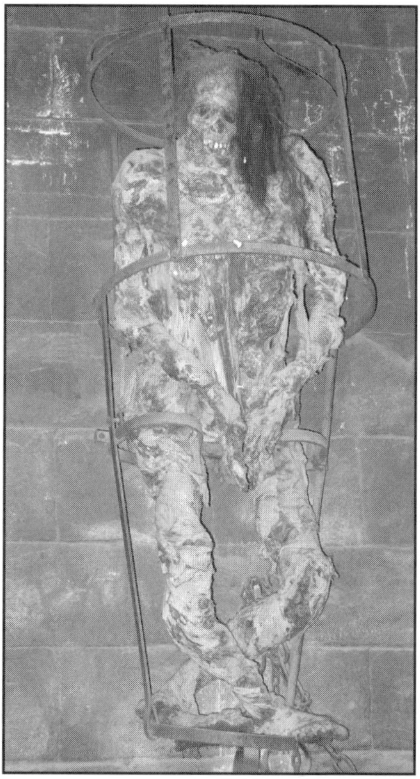

Life in medieval London was hard.
*Courtesy of D. Peter Lund*

# Haunted London

## English Ghosts, Legends, and Lore

E. Ashley Rooney

Schiffer® Publishing Ltd

4880 Lower Valley Road, Atglen, Pennsylvania 19310

**Cover photo:**
London 261. © Chris Harvey. Image from BigStockPhoto.com.



Library of Congress Control Number: 2008936384



Designed by Stephanie Daugherty

Type set in Butron's Nightmare 2000/ Arrus BT

ISBN: 978-0-7643-3149-7

Printed
in the United States of America



Published by Schiffer Publishing Ltd.
4880 Lower Valley Road
Atglen, PA 19310
Phone: (610) 593-1777
Fax: (610) 593-2002
E-mail: Info@schifferbooks.com



In Europe, Schiffer books are distributed by
Bushwood Books
6 Marksbury Ave.
Kew Gardens
Surrey TW9 4JF England
Phone: 44 (0) 20 8392-8585
Fax: 44 (0) 20 8392-9876
E-mail: info@bushwoodbooks.co.uk
Website: www.bushwoodbooks.co.uk
Free postage in the U.K., Europe; air mail at cost.

# GHOSTS

Many ghosts wander the streets of London. Sometimes the stories of these ghosts are not known. Often their stories are known, however. Some may still hope to change the face of history. Others are looking to recapture that special moment. These ghostly tales endeavor to give these spirits a past and perhaps even a future.

# Roots

*One tradition says that ghostly cries haunt a bend of the Thames River beneath where the London Bridge once stood.*

I've never been much of a practicing Jew nor have my parents. We show up at the temple on the big occasions: Yom Kippur, Rosh Hashanah, and Passover. We eat bacon, pork, and shrimp and mix dairy and meat, except when we visit my grandfather. He keeps kosher, which isn't easy to do when you are 72, he tells me. He buys only kosher, keeps his "Milchigs" and "Fleishigs," as he calls dairy and meat, separate and organizes them by a color scheme!

My mother says, "Bless his heart, Dad is from the old school. He wants to keep kosher, but I believe it is divisive."

"In what way?"

"It separates us from others—the Christians. I think breaking bread together breaks down those barriers between "us" and "them." At our Seder, we invite guests. How will we ever come together, if we don't share our stories?"

Whatever. I adore my grandpa. A professor of Jewish history, he tells me stories about our heritage. For him, Jews have always been persecuted and plundered, tormented and tortured, mutilated and massacred. He doesn't just focus on the Holocaust but goes all the way back to William the Conqueror. "Everybody talks about the Holocaust, but what happened there has happened for generations. And we always think that it's the Germans, but it isn't just the Germans. It's everybody – even the English."

"Really? I thought they were always friendly."

"No, they were as bad as the rest of them."

"Like what did they do, Grandpa?"

"I'm going back to the beginning," he warned. His eyes were deep-set and so sad, his beard longer than fashionable.

"There speaks my favorite history professor," I laughed.

"It's always easier to understand when you begin at the beginning, Sonia. William the Conqueror needed dues or taxes paid to him in coin rather than in kind."

"Why so?" I yawned.

"It took coins – not bushels of wheat – to meet his military requirements and build those big cathedrals. He needed moneylenders, but the Church frowned on usury. We Jews could meet his need."

"So that was good, wasn't it? It gave the Jews jobs."

"But not a popular job. No one likes a money lender."

"So did it give us anything else?"

"Well, initially, we were under the King's protection, but we were quite separate from the rest of the population. We didn't participate in the defense of the country, in the guilds or local government. Our worship services were different as was our day of worship. We couldn't eat food prepared by non-Jews, and, of course, we slaughtered animals according to religious teachings. Lending money further accentuated our differences." He brushed his beard slowly. I thought of my mother saying that keeping kosher separated us one from another. He continued, "When wealthy lords could not repay their loans, they could blame the Jewish moneylenders. When the King needed more money in his treasury, he could demand an additional tax from the moneylenders. As we prospered, the Christians became suspicious and envious. We were the minority. Why should we do well at their expense?" He sadly fondled his beard.

"So what happened?"

He looked up. "Once the Crusades began, however, we were subjected to more prejudice. To rouse the passions of the crusaders, Christian leaders told tales about infidels massacring men and women, circumcising Christians, and using Christian blood in odd rites."

I shivered. "Did they think Jews would suck their blood like vampires?"

"No, that's this century where you kids all talk about vampires and such. Back then it was all different. The Jews were non-Christians living right on the doorsteps of these would-be soldiers of the Cross. The Christian leaders spread rumors about ritual murders – you know the kind – like Jews killing Christian babies to make matzos from their blood."

"That's brutal. So what happened?"

"Throughout Europe, these zealous crusaders destroyed large communities of Jews. Their Christian leaders stirred their antipathy towards Jews into a positive burning hatred. Today, you would call it a pogrom."

My mother entered the room. "Dad, you'll be giving her nightmares, if you keep this up. She's only seventeen, after all."

"Oh, Mom," I said. "I like hearing his stories. After all, I am his youngest grandchild."

"That's right, Sonia." He rumpled my hair. Turning to Mother, he said, "It's important that she understands her heritage, dear, especially if you are taking her to London this summer."

"There are many other things in London: the National Gallery, Harrods, St. Paul's..."

"But London is a font of history, and our history is a part of it," he interrupted. "It wasn't just the twentieth century when Jews were not welcomed. In medieval times, the only reason the Jews were tolerated was because the Kings found that they had well-lined pockets. They taxed the Jews and made them pay for rights, which they freely gave to Christians.

If the Jews couldn't pay their dues, they were imprisoned in the Tower's Elephant House."

"An Elephant House?"

"Yes, it was built to house elephants. Beasts of burden. Now it housed Jews."

Mom interrupted. "Why don't you two go for a walk? Fresh air will be good for you, Dad. Ever since Mom died, you sit inside, remembering all this gloomy history. The sun is shining, the daffodils are almost out...."

"I want to finish my story. Will you listen, Sonia?" Mom groaned and left the room.

"Of course, Grandpa," I sat down. Mom was his only child. Now that Grandma had died, he had no one but our family to care about him. My older brothers and sisters were off at college or working so now only Mom, Dad and I were around to listen to Grandpa and his stories.

"In 1189, the bold swashbuckling Richard I was crowned King at Westminster Abbey. Some of the leading Jews traveled to London with its narrow streets, busy marketplaces and countless churches to bring presents for the new King."

"Just like the Magi," I exclaimed.

He nodded. "They couldn't go into the ceremony; it was considered a sacrilege for a Jew to be admitted to a Christian place of worship since they might exercise sorcery on the participating Christians. So the group of Jews mingled with others outside the gates of church. When some were pushed through the gates, the guards beat them for trying to enter the abbey. Suddenly, it became a riot. Every Jew to be found was beaten, and many killed. When the Jews ran to their houses, the crowd attacked them, setting their homes on fire and burning the inhabitants. The mayhem, plunder and killings became so violent that Christian attacked Christian. Although Richard I tried to stop the riot and protect the Jews, exaggerated stories spread throughout the country of the great riches that Christians had acquired from plundering the Jews."

"And then everyone wanted to get in on the act, right Grandpa?"

"Just about."

"Ok, Dad," my mother snapped. "That's enough. I don't want Sonia hearing all these awful stories."

"I thought you had left the room."

"I did, but I came back. " My mother retorted, "to find you still telling these bloodthirsty tales. There will never be any peace if you keep bringing up the past."

"But these are your ancestors too, dear. I keep telling you we need to understand our roots."

"And I keep telling you we need to move on – to forget the past!" Mom turned to me "Listen, Sonia, you've been asked to the prom, and now's the time to go shopping for that prom dress. We had better get looking! Goodbye Dad." And off we went to find the perfect dress and shoes. Luckily for me, my sister's hand-me-down was too big for me.

That night, as I stood in front of my steamed-up mirror, I began thinking about the prom and how I would look in my new blue dress with its low neckline. I began playing with my hair, pulling it up, putting it back, when an odd reflection appeared in the rainbow-covered mist. As I peered through the mist, I saw a young girl about my age and coloring. She was pretty, although she wore a cap covering most of her hair. I hastily wiped off the mirror to see more, but she faded away.

Of course, once my mother had said I was too young to listen to these tales of Jewish history, I wanted to hear more, but it wasn't until Mother's Day when we saw Grandpa again. This time, I took my mother's advice and suggested that he and I go for a walk. The walk was just to the end of his garden, where he sat in the evenings, watching the moon rise above the trees, listening to the rustle of nocturnal creatures. In the house, my older brothers and sisters were laughing as they prepared Sunday supper. As Grandpa and I sat there in the twilight, listening to the gentle cooing of the morning doves, I saw that girl again. She was standing on the deck of a ship. There was a smell of salt air; wind was flapping the sails. Seagulls were mewing overhead. I gasped. "Grandpa, do you see her?" "See whom?" he asked.

"Over there. That girl." It was the girl I had seen in my mirror. Her dress was floor length, loosely fitted, with long, tight sleeves and a narrow belt. Over this she wore a sleeveless vest. She slowly melted away into the dusk.

"No, I just see you. You must be dreaming."

"Maybe." I didn't think he was right. She seemed too real.

"Do you want me to tell you more about the Crusades?"

"I guess."

"It was a brutal time. When Richard left the country at the end of the twelfth century to join the Third Crusade, he left behind a people who were eager to pillage, persecute and massacre whole Jewish communities. The church wasn't going to protect them. The King wasn't there. Many Jews perished, and entire Jewish communities were wiped out.

"One of the worst incidents occurred in York, England. In 1190, the small Jewish community of York gathered together inside the castle for protection from the mob. Rather than perish at the hands of the violent mob that awaited them outside, some 150 mothers, fathers and children chose to die by each other's hands rather than abandon their faith. Those who finally surrendered were massacred."

Home in my own bed that night, I dreamed of burning houses and angry crowds. I saw flames and bodies. People kept yelling. Then I saw the girl again. She was standing on a sandy beach now, with the wind whipping her hair. Others were standing around her. They looked confused.

I didn't see Grandpa until later in the spring at my graduation. He gave me a string of pearls and a big hug. He had even trimmed his beard for the occasion. Two nights before Mom and I were to go to London, Grandpa and I had supper together. He was so proud of himself. He had ordered two kosher meals for us and since he knew I was a vegetarian he had selected tofu strips, marinated, sautéed with peppers, scallions, water chestnuts and baby corn. "See," he said, poking at the pan, "it comes topped with a Szechwan sauce, which I hope isn't too spicy for us, and there's steamed brown rice."

"I'm sure it will be fine." We sat at his kitchen table, and I told him what Mom and I planned to do in London for a week.

"After all our discussions, are you considering going to services there? I know you will see St. Paul's and Westminister Abbey, but how about checking out the local synagogue?"

"Maybe, Grandpa, but there's so much that we are trying to do in a short week."

"Oh," he fondled his beard. Guilt, guilt. But I wasn't going to take up precious time by going to a Jewish service. "So tell me more about the Jews in England," I asked.

"By 1218, every Jew in England had to wear a white badge. The towns began to restrict them from living within their limits, and the Jews were taxed more and more. Many were reduced to begging. Late in that century, a statute was passed that outlawed all usury, but, of course, the Jews couldn't suddenly become merchants or farmers because of the guilds. They were reduced to utter misery. The handwriting was on the wall, as they say."

"You mean it was time for them to leave town."

"You got it, Sonia. Edward I, known as the Hammer of the Scots spent a lot of money on his abortive Scottish campaigns and his Welsh castle building program. In 1290, Parliament gave him a large subsidy and, in turn, Edward I ordered all English Jews expelled."

"How many were there?"

"About three thousand. They could take their movable property, but the Crown seized all their estates, and all outstanding debts payable to Jews were transferred to the King's name. Edward supposedly got about two thousand pounds in proceeds from the houses they abandoned."

"That's awful. What did they do?"

"Some were killed. Many were robbed, and most tried to leave England. If they could pay, a ship would get them out of the country."

"So was that the end?"

"Not really. Nothing ever really ends. Life keeps going on, and often we don't learn from our mistakes."

"But why did people dislike Jews so?"

"Well, Sonia, their spiritual leaders, the priests, spoke out against them in the streets and churches. They were called sinners because they didn't believe in Jesus. They were the ones who lent money at interest, but was that their fault?"

"You said the Church and the laws of the land forced them into money lending."

"You have listened well. But perhaps your mother is right. The Jews didn't help the issue by living apart from the Christians. If they had tried to become acclimated, would it have been better?"

"Oh Grandpa, I'd like to think so."

Mom and I went to London. We stayed near St. James and took the tube everywhere. We were up early, playing tourist, and into bed late. We had tea at Kensington, stood with one leg in the East and one in the West at the observatory in Greenwich, saw the regimental band marching out of the

Guards' Barracks at Buckingham Palace, visited the Tower where we loved the stories of the Beefeaters, saw several shows, and went to Hampton Court for a day. We ate a ploughman's lunch, and I tried fish and chips. The chips were good; I still don't like fish that much. We had a great time, but one strange thing happened.

One misty evening we were going down the Thames towards Southwark Cathedral, where Old London Bridge had stood for many years. I heard these frantic voices calling. I looked around, but no one was to be seen. Then I saw the girl again. She was standing on a sandbar, tears rolling down her face. She was waving and pointing. I grabbed my mother's elbow. "Do you see her, Mom? Out there?"

"See who, dear? There's nothing out there but water."

"No, over there." But as I pointed, my vision – what else should I call her – faded away.

When I came home, I visited with Grandpa. After I told him about our trip, I hesitated and said, "There was this one weird thing."

"What was that?"

So I told him about how I had seen the girl several times. And how this time I had heard people calling to me. He nodded and said, "Your ancestors have reached out to you. Sit next to me, Sonia." He reached out and took my hand in his old wrinkled hand. And he told me one last story about the expulsion of the Jews from England.

"The Jews in London departed on St. Dennis Day. I am told that is October 9, 1290. Those who were rich arranged that a ship should take them and their immediate possessions to the Continent. When the ship was under sail and on the Thames beyond Queensborough, the shipmaster told his men to drop the anchor so the ship ran aground on dry sand. Then he told everyone, the expelled Jews and

The Thames River is much more crowded today than it was in 1290.
*Courtesy of D. Peter Lund*

the sailors, to stretch their legs on land. When he knew the tide was coming in, he gathered his sailors together and they went back to the ship, leaving the Jews. They cried to him for help, but he told them to cry instead to Moses who had conducted their forefathers through the Red Sea. Perhaps Moses would help them out of the rising water as the tide advanced. Then he sailed off. The Jews cried out, but no aid appeared. They drowned as the tide continued to rise."

He held my hand and said, "The story is told that if you are Jewish and have a special empathy you can hear the voices of the drowning Jews on the River Thames. Their agony persists through the generations." Raising his silver brows, he looked at me with his sad eyes, "One day the wolf shall dwell with the lamb, and the leopard shall lie down with the kid, but that day hasn't come yet."

**Author's Note:** The majority of the Jews seem to have crossed the channel in safety. A few indispensable Jewish doctors were said to have remained behind, but most Jews preferred exile to renouncing their faith. They were not formally readmitted into England until about four centuries later under Oliver Cromwell.

**Directions:** Exit the Monument Underground Station to Fish Street and go left on Lower Thames until you reach the stairs that lead to the London Bridge. You will see a gap in the skyline to your left, which is where the Old London Bridge stood.

# She Wolf

In the Middle Ages and the Renaissance, women were not considered equal. People believed that they had neither the intellect nor the character required to be a good leader. A woman was expected to marry in order to produce heirs and guarantee the succession. If a female ruler were to marry, she could place her realm in a highly vulnerable position.

*She-Wolf of France, with unrelenting fangs,*
*That tear'st the bowels of thy mangled mate.*
Thomas Gray, "The Bard"

Today, I walk this small graveyard, holding his heart in a silver casket – that's the only way I'll ever hold my husband's heart. Once I wore rustling silks and cloth of gold. I had jewels, lands, and healthy children. I was beautiful with long blonde hair and striking features inherited from my mother, Johanna of Navarre. Now, I am just crumbling dust and a shadow on moonlit nights. But let me start at the beginning.

A princess, I was the sister to three princes and the only surviving daughter of Philip IV of France, which meant I was his pawn on the diplomatic chessboard. My father arranged a marriage between Edward II, the first English prince to hold the title Prince of Wales, and me to seal the peace between our two countries. He announced: "You are a valuable tool for developing alliances between Kings and kingdoms. You have no say in it because these are the affairs of men." Looking back, I realize I traded one lord for another – both of whom I was meant to obey. Like Father said, I had no say in it. But women's feelings and thoughts didn't count for much in those days. And princesses, well, we were ladies in the tower – the object of favors from gallant knights. We were to smile sweetly, look demure, marry whomever our parents selected for us and raise heirs to the throne – all of which I did. But I did more and became known as the She Wolf. That's why I'm in this churchyard with my husband's heart in my hand.

I was twelve when I married tall, slim, 24-year-old Edward II with his hair of gold. He looked just like one of the princes in my cherished tales of courtly romance. I was a King's daughter marrying a King, who would love me forever. He was God's anointed, and we would rule England together. Eight Kings and Queens were present at our marriage in Boulogne; my crown glittered with jewels; and I wore a brilliant blue and gold gown with a red mantle. The music played, the food was elegant, the drink lavish. Of course, at age 12, I didn't know that not everything is as it seems, but there were many things I didn't know then.

I had everything I could possibly need: a handsome husband, who was a King, and many crowns, jewels and dishes. My chests were full of gold and silver, velvet and silk dresses, furs and seventy-two headdresses. But as soon as we disembarked at the famous white cliffs of Dover, Edward ran off the ship, running to this dark handsome man, embracing him with great enthusiasm and calling him brother. He then gave him – this stranger – my favorite wedding present! I wanted to stomp my foot, but I knew I had to act like I didn't mind.

As I told my children later, image matters a great deal when you are royalty. To control men accustomed to power and military action, you have to be a strong leader—or so I learned from my father. Edward's fatal flaw was that he was not a good leader in battle or at home. He liked to row and swim; he enjoyed common pursuits such as digging and building walls; his friends were singers and actors; and he certainly had neither the maturity nor the experience to deal with the continual battles with the Scots and the always empty royal coffers. On the other hand, he knew how to give his special friend, Piers Gaveston, lavish gifts. He also knew how to ignore the warnings of his elders or the advice of his counselors.

We entered London on February 19, 1308, with cheering crowds, a four-mile long procession, and many splendid pageants. My royal apartments were at the Tower of London, and our coronation took place that month. It wasn't a happy event. Having been given the responsibility for planning the event, the flamboyant Piers gave himself a major role, almost eclipsing Edward and certainly surpassing the other earls. Already envious of him, they were displeased to say the least. He took all the major roles such as carrying the crown and fastening the King's spurs, which made Edward's nobles seethe. Piers even wore robes of purple trimmed with pearls instead of the cloth of gold worn by his fellow peers, and everyone knows that purple is a color reserved for the King. What disturbed me was that Edward chose to sit with Piers rather than with me, his Queen.

My relatives noting that Edward had his arms arrayed alongside that of Piers – not mine– were appalled. They declared that my husband, the King, preferred Piers' couch to mine! I thought to myself that when I was older that the situation would be different.. Edward would prefer my couch!

All in all, it was a huge disaster. There weren't enough chairs so the nobility had to stand. It took too long, and it was almost evening before anyone ate that enormous banquet of salted and fresh fish, snipes, quails and partridge, marchpane, gingerbread and cakes.

By the time I was fifteen, Edward had come to my bed, and I was pregnant! Edward began to treat me as his Queen. I had a household of over two hundred people and owned large estates, jewels and many precious things. As mother of the future heir to the throne, my position was now established, but the Scots kept rebelling and the barons didn't respect Edward. The barons attempted to bring him under control by a series of ordinances designed to limit his power. That same year, 1312, the Earl of Lancaster and his baronial allies captured Piers, claiming that he led the King to folly. They killed him.

Edward was devastated. Secretly rejoicing that now I had no rival for his affections, I comforted him. I told him to restore the barons' estates, quench the rebellions on our borders and convince his subjects that he was truly their King. The same year I had my first son, Edward III, at Windsor Castle. Once I was strong enough, we celebrated his birth with a procession and a pageant by the Fishmonger's Guild in London.

By 1319, I had a wealthy household, a host of retainers, many estates and three healthy children – something that many of my contemporaries did not. Edward gave me jewels, cloths of gold and Turkish carpets. We were content. Now Piers was gone, Edward was mine. I was his favorite. All was favorable until we were defeated at Bannockburn and driven from Scotland. The treasury was empty again, but the country could not afford to abandon the north to Scottish raids.

But then Edward met the Despensers, father and son, who wormed their way into his favor. Suddenly, Hugh the Younger was exchanging secret smiles with Edward and voicing his opinions about matters of state. My foolish Edward smiled back and gave him extravagant gifts. From then on, anything Hugh wanted he got, and my bed was empty again! Fortunately for me, Edward's baronial opponents demanded that the Despensers be exiled because of their growing influence over the King. The elder Despenser went into hiding, and the younger turned to piracy in the English Channel. When the pair returned, many Englishmen were robbed of their lands and estates, and corruption was endemic. There was a storm of hatred for the Despensers, both father and son, and the barons revolted again, but they were crushed and Edward's chief opponent, Lancaster, was executed in 1322. Many others were hung, drawn and quartered, and their children and wives imprisoned. Crippling fines were demanded, and no one felt safe from Edward's whim or Despenser greed.

The Despensers ruled England through Edward, their puppet. At the York Parliament of 1322, Edward issued a statute, which formally annulled all previous ordinances designed to make him subject to the will of Parliament. Some call this time the "tyranny." Edward decked the Despensers with prizes stolen from his barons, and the three of them had a gay old time. The lords of the land, the tradesmen and even common Englishmen were offended: their King was corruptible and easily swayed by his favorites. I burned with rage, but I knew better than to display it. I just needed to bide my time and keep a smile on my face.

The situation became so bad that Edward and I lived separate lives. I no longer exercised patronage, received gifts, or enjoyed any of the valuables taken by the Despensers as they terrorized the land. By 1324, the King had taken away all of my lands and ordered the arrest and imprisonment of all Frenchmen in England as well as confiscation of their property. Then he took my younger children and entrusted them to the Despensers. I seethed, as did the country, but I tried not to show my hatred for the Despensers. Meanwhile, the French and Flemish were waiting for an opportunity to wage war on English soil, the Scots were rallying in the north, the Welsh rebelling in the west, and, of course, there were always the Irish.

Fortunately, my brother, Charles IV of France, began to be annoyed by Edward's refusal to pay homage for the territory of Gascony. Edward decided that I was the best person to represent his interests. Certainly, his obedient wife would do as told. I nodded submissively. Overjoyed, I arrived in France in March 1325, where I agreed to a peace treaty, favoring France and requiring Edward to pay homage in France. Then he sent my 13-year-old son, Edward, to pay homage instead. What a stupid mistake! I was in possession of the King's heir, my son!

Tired of being quiet and demure, I decided I had been humiliated long enough. I had a brain, a heart, emotions, and I was now free to use them. Dressing myself in widow's weeds, I proclaimed loudly, "Someone has come between my husband and myself trying to break this bond. I protest that I will not return until this intruder has been removed, but, discarding my marriage garment, I shall assume the robes of widowhood and mourning." Of course, Despenser was that someone, and most of Europe knew it.

My estates were no longer mine. My fortune was not mine. I only had my name and even that was stained by the knowledge that Edward sought another in his bed (and a man at that!). But by this time so did I. The exiled Roger Mortimer, an ambitious Welsh baron and a seasoned warrior, and I were lovers. To me, he was everything that Edward was not: virile, courageous and decisive. He had even escaped from the Tower by a rope ladder, crossing the Thames and fleeing England. I know I risked society condemning us for our double adultery for we both were married – but I had had enough! Only twenty-nine years old, I had spent seventeen years with a man who preferred undeserving sycophants who wormed their way into his favor.

In September of 1326, Prince Edward, Mortimer and I invaded England. Few people were prepared to fight for Edward II. We easily vanquished the royal forces, capturing Edward and the Despensers. On October 27, the elder Despenser was accused of encouraging the illegal government of his son, enriching himself at the expense of others, despoiling

World War II bombings destroyed Christ Church Greyfriars, also known as Christ Church Newgate, but the pretty churchyard contains several tombs. *Courtesy of D. Peter Lund*

the Church, and taking part in the illegal execution of the Earl of Lancaster. He was hung, drawn and quartered, and his head sent to Winchester. Hugh Despenser was charged with many crimes, including maliciously interfering in our marriage, forcing me from my lands, and many other complaints. The assembled lords and knights quickly convicted him of treason. He was to be hung, castrated, drawn and quartered. A terrible death, but he deserved it. Afterwards, I rewarded my supporters with monies seized from his household, restored lands, opened prisons and attempted to alleviate the pain of his victims.

Eventually, Parliament agreed to depose the King and replace him with our son, Edward III, who was underage. The abdication was announced and recorded in London on January 24, 1327. I had won! I had led a successful invasion of England, deposed the King and established myself as regent for my young son. I busied myself acquiring lands and treasure. But within a year, sympathy began to grow for my husband, who was engaged in writing poetry. Typical!

When I thought about it, I didn't need Edward. As King, he was not well liked. As a prisoner, he was an embarrassment. We moved Edward from Kenilworth to Berkeley Castle, near the Welsh March. There he died. People say that our agent killed him by inserting a red-hot iron rod into his rectum. Some say that Mortimer killed him without my permission. Some say that our letter to his jailers asking them to take care that no one kill him was misread. Defeating rumors is like wrestling with shadows. You never know the truth for sure.

By 1330, Wales was discontented, exiles were plotting an invasion, and London and adjacent areas were uneasy. The King was dead, and Edmund, Earl of Kent, the half-brother of Edward II, was executed under strange circumstances. When my son, Edward III became age 18 in 1330, he and several compatriots overthrew our regime and took Mortimer and me prisoner. Despite my cries of "*Fair son, have pity on gentle Mortimer,*" my lover was hanged for treason, and his vast estates forfeited to the crown.

My son allowed me to retire to Castle Rising in Norfolk. I visited Edward and Philippa's court often, where I spent time with my grandchildren: Edward, The Black Prince, John of Gaunt, Lionel of Antwerp, Edmund of Langley and Thomas of Woodstock. I received a constant stream of gifts and had minstrels, eight ladies of the chamber, thirty-three clerks and squires. I owned many jewels and lovely clothes. They say the Queen is the most powerful and feared piece on the chessboard. That's true – if she takes control of her destiny. We have both our sexuality and our intelligence, which we can use to our ends. And I did that finally!

I chose Greyfriers, the Franciscan church at Newgate, as my last resting place. Built in 1225, this Gothic church is the second largest in medieval London. I was buried there along with Marguerite of France, the second wife of King Edward I, and the heart of Eleanor of Provence, wife of Henry III. I was buried in my wedding dress, with Edward's heart in a casket on my breast. Finally, his heart is mine. People say that I can be seen walking the park clutching the silver casket. I won't let it go. A Queen deserves a King. And despite my father's best efforts, I never really had Edward II.

**Directions:** Greyfriars Churchyard is on the corner of Newgate Street and King Edward Street. World War II bombings destroyed Christ Church Greyfriars, also known as Christ Church Newgate, but the pretty churchyard has several tombs.

# The Plague of 1348

*Charterhouse Park is a lovely green space in the middle of London. It offers a place to sit and watch the birds, to read a newspaper, to share a bite of lunch with a friend. It also is the burial place for about 5,000 victims of the Black Death or the plague in 1348. In London as in other great European cities, when the plague came, pits were dug and piled high with the dead. As soon as those pits were filled, more were dug. No one wept for anyone who died, for all awaited death during the plague years. So many died unmourned, without a funeral, without last rites, that chroniclers of the time saw it as a sign that the end of the world was imminent. Even today, if you wander the nearby streets at night, you can hear the voices of the dead beseeching you to at least mourn for them.*

My name is Edmund Connor. I am a teacher here in London. When people die in my local parish, I record the names of the dead and the date that they are buried. If I am lucky, I get paid. This year has been very different because many have died this summer. People have buried their family members, neighbors, friends, customers and employees.

With so many dead, civilization seems to be dying too. People just walk into empty houses and take whatever they want. They quarrel over the property of the dead, and when children are orphaned their elders vie to adopt the heir. The fields lie untilled, the livestock roam the hills, and food is meager. The dead are thrown in deep trenches and covered with a scattering of dirt. No one says prayers for the dead – most of whom have died without having a chance to confess their sins.

They say it is the plague, which started in the East, possibly China, and quickly spread throughout Europe. This deadly pestilence has wiped out whole communities;

in some areas, corpses litter the streets because no one is left to bury them. When the plague came to England, it spread quickly through the crowds at market. It leapt from there to the taverns, from the visitors to the townspeople, from the poor to the wealthy – unless they left town in time. They say it begins with apple-size swellings under the arm or in the groin, and then there is a purplish-black rash and hemorrhaging. The victims smell terribly and suffer severe pain. My wife Nancy agonizes about our only child Robert. He's ten years old and our pride and joy.

"He can't get it," she cries. "He can't, Edmund. He's all we have."

I hug her tightly, appreciating the heat of her body. "And we will keep him safe, Nancy. Don't you worry." Through her light wool shift, my fingertips explore the muscles of her back, the bones of her ribs and the softness of her waist.

But I don't really how we can keep Robert safe. We live on one of the nicer cobblestone streets lined with comfortable timber frame houses thatched with straw. Shops occupy the ground floors, and the owners live above. Not far from here – maybe a ten minutes' walk — the area is overcrowded and unsanitary. People sleep with their animals: their cows, pigs, sheep and chickens under one roof. One bed often accommodates all family members. Rushes thick with vermin cover the floors. There the bones and food remains are thrown to the dogs. The streets are muddy most of the time, and open gutters carry the waste, including excrement and the blood of slaughtered animals, to the Thames. Garbage rots in the streets while vermin forage for food. The stench is overpowering.

I talk to my friend Richard, the tavern keeper. He says, "Why worry, Edmund. You too will soon be dead. It's like the Bible says; we should enjoy life as much as possible because it will soon be over. You might as well have another glass of ale and enjoy yourself. Certainly, you don't want to drink any water, which could be infested with frogs and other worms."

"Ah," I say, "Give me another drink then. So you espouse the Italian philosophy of 'Eat, drink and be merry, for tomorrow you may die?"'

"Yes." He bangs down his glass. "Why run around wondering what you can do to avoid it? Why not just enjoy the days you have left together with your family and friends."

I go home and take Nancy and Robert to the market. It's not as populated as it has been, but traveling musicians, maimed beggars and dancing bears crowd the streets. A friar in long robes preaches about hell's fire. We laugh and forget the world about us. When we return home, Nancy has supper for us: bacon boiled with leeks, yellow cheese, new bread, red apples and wine from Gascony. When Robert goes to bed, we do too.

Three days later, my neighbor tells me that he has heard that Richard has the plague. "His thirst is unquenchable; he bleeds from everywhere." My neighbor's breath smells bad. I move away from him.

I go to see my friend Martin. I ask him what he is doing to avoid the plague.

Shaking his fist in my face, he proclaims, "God has sent the plague to punish us for our sins. It is his righteous retribution raining down like arrows from the sky in judgment of man's greed, heresy and dissent."

"Do you truly believe that the plague is the will of God?"

"I do indeed. People question the authority of God's holy church and its ministers. They doubt the sacrament. God is angry, and his rage is fierce. He will find you – no matter where you hide."

"So is there anyone I can pray to?"

"You should ask yourself what sins you have committed to merit such a punishment. Then confess your sins, fast, pray and lead a better life. And may God have mercy on your soul."

Coming home on the narrow, dirty streets, stinking of decaying offal, I hold my nose. The ditch by the side of the road is filled with refuse from homes, slaughterhouses and stables. Although the Corporation of London forbade any citizen to throw dust, dung, sawdust, straw or other garbage into the streets, many do – along with the contents of chamber pots.

On Wednesday, the plague struck a family two streets away. Nancy asks whether there is any treatment. "There is no cure," I tell her. "None that works anyway." She tells me that her friend Abigail believes that the air transmits the disease so she burns fragrant woods such as pine or juniper and covers her face with cloths dipped in aromatic oils when leaving the house. Nancy burns rosemary incense and makes nosegays of flowers for us to wear around our necks.

She says that her friend Mary told her that under no circumstances should she take a bath because it will open up the pores of the body to the infected air. Then she says that her friend told her sleeping on the back – the way I do – is the worst position because the poisonous air descends through the nostrils to the lungs. I laugh when she tells me this, and she storms off. We are all a bit on edge. I would have bought her a charm or a spell from the apothecary to make her happy, but he died last week. Guess those charms didn't work very well for him.

People tell me terrible stories of what happens with the plague. Entire families die. Cattle roam the streets. Unburied bodies rot in empty houses. If there are no wagons for the dead, members of a household bring their dead to a ditch as best as they can and throw dirt over them. I think to myself I need to know how to cure this disease if, God forbid, we get it. I know what to do if someone is burned or what herbs to give them if they are nauseated – hawkweed and sorrel – but the plague is a mysterious thing.

I go to my friend John, who knows something of medicine. "What can we do?"

"You can use leeches to remove infected blood and restore the balance of your humors."

"But that doesn't seem to work either."

"No, there is little anyone can do to escape death's onslaught." John sighs. He's old now – somewhere in his late forties — and all his teeth have fallen out, but he's still the best physician I know. "Some think you can escape it."

"How?"

"It seems to leap from one person to another. So you should stay home as much as possible, or board a ship and go overseas or go to the country and stay away from people."

I go home and tell Nancy to seal the windows and doors so we can keep the corrupted air at bay. We tell our servant to go elsewhere. I tell Nancy to stay at home with Robert. "Avoid the markets, the common wells and social gatherings. Leave early, go far and stay long. That's what the rich folks do. You could leave for your parents today."

"Oh, but I'm not ready. I have to gather our belongings, say goodbye to your parents. Maybe tomorrow."

The next day, when I wake up Nancy, she's perspiring. I place my hand on her forehead. She rolls away from me. "Oh, I have such a headache, Edmund."

"I'm sorry." I stroke her head. Her eyes look dazed. Her skin feels clammy.

"I can't leave when I feel like this. Let me sleep for awhile, and I will be fine." She closes her eyes.

Four hours later, I wake her up again. "Nancy, It's time for you to get going if you're going to get anywhere before night."

She groans. "I feel awful."

"Any pains?" I ask.

"My groin has a dreadfully tender place."

My heart falls. The buboes are often found in the armpit or the groin. "Let me look," I say.

She begins to cough in her hand. When she takes her hand away from her mouth, I see blood. I lie her back down. "Here, you rest. I'll get you some water."

Two days later, Nancy is sweating steadily. Her nose trickles blood. The buboes ooze steadily; the stench is gross. A rash of purplish black spots encircles her slender neck. She's dying. My pretty Nancy, the mother of my son. We've lived together for fifteen years, and she's dying in five days. Who would guess? When she dies, I wrap her body in a bloody sheet. At night we bring her corpse out when we hear the cry, "Bring out your dead." Her body, which I have slept with for so many years, is thrown on the cart and taken away to the plague pit, where if she is lucky someone will throw some dirt upon it. She didn't even have a chance to make confession.

The rich and the poor, women and men, children and adults, are all dumped into the trench, and dirt is scattered on top of them. During the day, crows and vultures settle there. When a human approaches, they swarm up into the sky, circling and hovering, waiting for feeding time to begin again. As the bodies begin to rot, a foul stench creeps into the area.

That night, I dream that Nancy comes to my bed. She sits down on its edge. Her familiar face is transparent. The moonlight shines through her as she leans forward to kiss me. I hold out my arms to her, and a buzzard comes in the room and pecks at her head. She disappears, and I lie there, cold and shaking.

The next day, I go to retrieve her body. I know that's what her spirit wants; she doesn't want to be there in that pit with everyone else. She wants to be home with me, where I can care for her and give her a proper funeral. I go to the pit, but I can't see her in that tangled mess of arms and legs. The brazen birds dare me to come closer. I can feel the wings of a buzzard above my head. They dart down as if they will attack me. Can they tell the difference between alive and dead? I leave, calling myself a coward.

When I come home, my father and mother are there, complaining about the piles of clothing, bedding and other furnishings belonging to plague victims that are piled into the street. Mother believes the city should burn them, but Father insists that if they burn the infected furnishings they will simply release the plague back into the air. They go to visit their friends.

Robert and I go to bed early that night. I hope that Nancy won't return, but she does. Tonight, an eerie mist shrouds her. She's crying. "Please Edmund, please bring me home. I'm alone there."

I turn over, trying to ignore her. She's just a ghost after all. She shakes my shoulder, "Help me, help me, Edmund. I am all alone." I hear the sound of crows outside the door. I stand up, and Nancy disappears. Someone is at the door. My parents have returned. Mother's face is wet with sweat, and she moves like she has been drinking. I lead her to the bench by the fireplace. Dropping onto the seat, she sighs heavily. She shudders frequently as if she is cold, but the back of her dress is wet with sweat. I bring her a pewter pitcher of cool water; she drinks three glassfuls, swallowing as if she cannot get enough. Her tongue is swollen and bright red. When she tries to get up, my father forces her back. She thrashes wildly, and I see the tender-looking red swelling in her armpit – the beginning of the bubo. When Robert appears at the door, I snap angrily at him and tell him to leave. A thick red mucus bubbles from her nose. Mother dies soon. Her tongue is black, and she has black blisters all over her body. I hear the gravediggers calling, "Bring out your dead." I open the window, and I see bodies, tossed every way, filling a cart: arms and legs, heads and buttocks. Mother's body joins them.

That night, Nancy returns. The moonlight shines through her. "Your Mother is with me now, Edmund." I try to ignore

When the streets near Charterhouse Park are still, you can hear the voices of the dead calling you from the 1348 plague pit buried under the park. During the plague, the dead were dumped into trenches and covered with a thin layer of dirt until the trench was full. *Courtesy of D. Peter Lund*

her woeful face. Birds are pecking on the roof above us. She says, "I'm leaving now, Edmund. We'll talk again." I turn over and put the pillow over my head.

London is changing day by day. Many shops have closed, and the vendors have disappeared from the streets. Now the streets are quiet. Friends avoid friends, shopkeepers are afraid of the customers and vice versa. Executions, puppet shows and even funerals are no more. All is quiet except for the bells, which continue to toll for the dead.

Two weeks later, my father, Robert, and I fell sick. They lie flat on their backs, eyes fixed and wide open but seeing nothing. I crawl around, trying to sponge the sweat off them. Within two days, we all have large painful buboes. Nancy sits by my side every night. My father and Robert have a vile smell. Probably I do, too. Our neighbor charges us to keep within the house – not that we could go anywhere, we feel so awful. He tells me that someone has painted a large red cross on the front door and the words "Lord have mercy on us."

The thirst is overpowering. I have a fever, but I can hear Robert's teeth chattering. I want to help him, but I can't move. The red bubo in my groin gets bigger and bigger. It shines in the light. When it bursts, the blood pours out in a thick scarlet stream. I scream at the horror of it, but all is quiet around me. I realize that everyone else has died. I was there on my bed while Father and Robert died. God preserved me. I'm not sure why. Their corpses just lay there until my neighbor comes by. "Phew," he spits. "It smells awful in here. Anyone still alive?" I groan.

I am still alive, but it is a harsh world. Now I am the one who is all alone – except at night when Nancy visits. The streets are empty; the houses of death are still; the only sound is that of the wheels of the death carts on their way to the plague pits, the calls of the scavengers and the voices of the dead. When the weather turns cold this January, the plague should go away. But it will come back.

**Author's Note:** On November 1, 1348, the plague reached London. Accounts say that up to 42 percent of the city's population of 70,000 inhabitants succumbed. There was no place to put all those bodies, so pits were dug.

Over the next two years, the plague is said to have killed between 30-40 percent of the entire English population. Given that the pre-plague population of England was in the range of 5-6 million people, fatalities may have reached as high as 2 million dead.

The plague did strike again. The Great Plague (1625-1631) was a massive outbreak that killed up to one fifth of London's population. There was no cure for it at that time.

**Directions:** Charterhouse Square is a pleasant park, which can be reached by the Barbican or Farringdon tube.

# The Bloodthirsty Time

*...look back with me unto the Tower.*
*Pity, you ancient stones, those tender babes,*
*Whom envy hath immured within your walls!*
*Rough cradle for such little, pretty ones!*
*Rude ragged nursed, old sullen playfellow*
*For tender princes...*
Shakespeare, *Richard III*, Act IV, Scene I

I've had a confusing life – probably not as confusing as my dashing father who seized the throne at age eighteen, while England was still suffering from the massive struggle between the Houses of Lancaster and York for the throne of England. You might know it better as the War of Roses, a most perplexing war with many characters.

In 1461, my father, Edward of York, who was famed for his kingship, his looks, and his generalship, became Edward IV through the support of his cousin, the Earl of Warwick or "The Kingmaker." Warwick planned that Edward should marry a French princess, but instead he married Elizabeth Woodville from a large ambitious Lancastrian family. Many made jokes about the greed of her family. As Father explained it later, "I wanted to marry the woman of my choice. I am King after all."

"Does that mean I can make a marriage of my choosing?"

"Whoa, son." He put one of his big arms around me and pulled me close. "I expect you to make a marriage that would be an asset to England—one that will bring money and powerful allies." His marriage didn't do that; it brought him grasping relatives, stepsons, and many children. In turn, he heaped favors on his new relatives, making other nobles, such as the Earl of Warwick, furious.

So Warwick and father's brother, the Duke of Clarence, led an army against Edward. Things got complicated then. When Father and his youngest brother Richard, Duke of Gloucester, escaped to the Low Countries in one of the many rebellions that tore England apart, the opposing army entered London. My mother and my three sisters, Elizabeth, Mary, and Cicely, along with some attendants, fled up the Thames to Westminister to a place called the Sanctuary, where I was born on November 1, 1470. We remained there with my three older sisters until Father invaded England early in March. That was the first time we met. Mother told me he was so excited because he now had an heir–me!–who would inherit the throne. Father deposed Henry VI, who had been restored to the throne for a brief time; Father took his throne back; and Henry was murdered. I should point out that the fifteenth century in England was a bloodthirsty time.

I became Prince of Wales in June 1471. In 1473, my father established my household at Ludlow Castle far to the west on the Welsh Marches. Of course, I didn't run it; I was only three years old after all! Instead of selecting one of his brothers, Father made Anthony Woodville, Earl Rivers, who was my mother's brother, my governor and put him in charge of my household. I was considered the nominal head of the Council of the Welsh Marshes, and orders were sent out in my name. Of course, I couldn't really appreciate all this.

That same year my brother Richard was born. He was created the Duke of York in 1475. Father appointed me Guardian of the Realm for the time he would be gone in France, and I was knighted at the Palace of Westminister. Much discussion ensued about my marrying the Spanish Infanta Isabella, but nothing came of it.

Westminister Abbey has been the coronation church since 1066 and almost all of the British monarchs have been crowned there. Many of the kings and queens of England and their consorts are buried here. The abbey also houses the tombs of famous poets, musicians, generals, admirals, politicians, scientists, doctors, and others. *Courtesy of D. Peter Lund*

My life was very organized. Father had big plans for me, his heir. I awoke each morning and attended Matins and mass before breakfast. My tutors instructed me all morning. Father considered book learning most important. I learned chivalry through history and stories and in practice through the knightly arts such as horsemanship, swordsmanship and jousting. Then we had Vespers and supper, where someone read to me. Finally, free time! The household officials, chaplains and schoolmasters taught me what it was to be a gentleman; to possess chivalry, courtliness, generosity and loyalty. Father ordered that I was to be surrounded with people of virtuous characters who were not to swear or use bad language.

My brother Richard, at age four, married Anne Mowbray, the infant heiress of the duchy of Norfolk, in January of 1477. Arras of gold hung in St. Stephen's chapel, Westminster, where the ceremony was performed. Mother led Richard, who was not five, and her brother, Earl Rivers, led three-year old Anne down the aisle. A big banquet followed. My Uncle Clarence, who had given Father some problems, died soon after that. People wouldn't talk about it, but I heard something about him falling into a barrel of malmsey. My cousins, Margaret and Edward (see "Off with That Head") came to live with my brother Richard and my sisters. My uncle Gloucester ruled the turbulent north in Father's name. I didn't see him much, but Father really liked him. He told me, "Your Uncle Richard led the thundering cavalry charges in all those battles."

"He was young then."

"Yes, but he was smart enough to scorn the French King's bribes. He was by my side throughout that time. He's a brother I can trust. Look how well he's handling the Scots border these days. That's the kind of brother I need."

I spent most of my time at Ludlow. In 1481, I toured Kent with Father, visiting St. Thomas Becket's shrine at

Canterbury, where the citizens presented me with a silver gilt box and 20 pounds, and reviewing Lord Howard's fleet at Sandwich. It felt good to be traveling with him. He was very popular and loved to show off how big and strong he was. Sometimes he embarrassed me because he was always looking at women. His eyes would wander down their bodice; he would smile into their eyes. They would wink at him, give long languishing looks, toss their hair back and giggle. I would get this uneasy feeling in my stomach.

When I was ten years old, Father negotiated an alliance in 1481 with the Duke of Brittany, Francis II, which involved my betrothal to the four-year-old, Anne, his daughter and heiress. She and a dowry of 200,000 crowns would be sent to England when she reached the age of twelve. When I married her, I would become the Duke of Brittany; our second son would inherit Brittany; our first would inherit England, of course.

But then Father got sick; on April 9, 1483, he died at age forty. My tall, strong father, whom everyone loved, was dead! I was always a bit scared of him, but he was a good father. I was just thirteen years old. Fast-riding messengers came to Ludlow to tell us. My mother, my brother Richard, and my sisters were in London. They also told us that Father's will appointed my uncle Gloucester Protector of the Realm and my guardian. While I was still in Ludlow, I was proclaimed King Edward V in London on April 11, 1483. By then, it was obvious that my Uncle Richard, Duke of Gloucester, did not like or trust my mother's family, the Woodvilles. They didn't like him either. But I knew that Father intended that Gloucester should govern the kingdom while I was a minor and have care and control of my siblings and me. I trusted Father's judgment and in Gloucester's faithful service. After all, his motto was "Loyaulte me Lie" (Loyalty Binds Me).

About two weeks later, Lord Rivers, a small armed guard and I set out for London. We met my half-brother, Lord Richard Grey, at Northampton and spent the night at Stony Stratford. Lord Rivers, who appeared somewhat worried, had dinner with Gloucester and Buckingham down the road. He never came home that night so the next morning, we set out for London without him. Suddenly, Uncle Richard and Buckingham rode up the road. They treated me like the King – even bending their knee!

Richard said, "I am so sorry that your father died. He was a good King and a great warrior."

"Thank you."

"When I heard, I arranged for a requiem mass at York, and in my hall the courtiers took an oath of loyalty to you."

"Thank you."

"You are the Lord's anointed King."

"Yes."

"But it's your mother's relatives who caused your father's death."

"What?"

"Yes, they were the "servants and companions of his vices" and ruined his health. They must be removed before they bring harm to you – England's new King."

"They wouldn't… I certainly can answer for Lord Rivers and Grey here that they are innocent."

Buckingham interjected, "You must be removed from the custody of your Woodville relatives for your own safety."

"They will bring harm to you. Already, they are planning to kill me so I can't be your protector as your father dictated," Gloucester said.

Grey began to protest, but Buckingham shouted, "Quiet!"

I couldn't believe what was happening. I said, "I don't know about my brother Dorset, but my Lord Rivers and my brother Grey are innocent of any such matter."

Buckingham sneered. "They have the dealing of these matters far from the knowledge of your Grace. There are hazards associated with a minor inheriting the throne."

I retorted, "I have faith in the peers of the realm and the Queen."

Buckingham said. "It is not the business of women but of men to rule kingdoms."

Gloucester arrested Grey and the other men of my household; they were sent to one of Gloucester's northern castles. He then dismissed my escort and replaced them with their men. I knew that further protest was useless. Gloucester had won, but I wasn't sure what it all meant for me. I'm afraid I wept then. Lord Rivers had been with me for a long time; he was gone and I didn't know where.

With a force of about five hundred soldiers, we rode for London. When we reached London on May 4, the scarlet-clad Lord Mayor, aldermen and sheriffs and mounted members of the great livery companies met me. Clad in blue velvet, I suddenly began to feel like a King after the confusion of the journey. My Uncle Richard, who wore black for my father, kept presenting me to the cheering crowds, saying "Behold your prince and lord." Gloucester gave orders for my coronation on June 22. Later various people swore their fealty to me.

There was a good deal of talk about where I should live. Finally, it was decided that the Tower of London was appropriate. In mid-May, I took the royal apartments situated on the south side of the White Tower, facing the River Thames. I had three rooms with stained glass windows. In the next several days, I learned how to be King. I was measured for my coronation clothes, signed documents and held meetings.

I wanted to see my mother, but I never did. She, my brother Richard and my sisters had left Westminster Palace for the Sanctuary before we even arrived in London. My half-brother Dorset gave up his role as constable of the Tower and also went to Sanctuary. I thought it odd that that Mother didn't come out of Sanctuary to see me.

I didn't have anyone I knew well with me. Gloucester was a stranger – he had spent most of his time up north before Father died. Mother and my sisters and brother were still in Sanctuary. Then Lord Hastings who had been a favorite of my father's was executed. My dreams left me sweating. I didn't know what was happening; my life seemed to be a vortex of intrigue. No one mentioned my coronation anymore. Did that mean there wouldn't be one? And what did that mean?

The Tower of London has been the scene of great intrigue, blood and death. William the Conqueror built the White Tower, the original stark square fortress, in 1078. Certainly, it has many ghosts. *Courtesy of D. Peter Lund*

Fortunately, my brother Richard joined me on June 16. I was no longer alone. He was too young to understand why I was afraid, but I was no longer alone. My brother was with me. We were moved to the White Tower with a different set of servants. I had a miserable toothache, but my real problem was I was scared. Sudden rushes of panic would sweep through me. In the middle of the night, I would wake up with the sweat chilling my body as the minutes ticked by. Sometimes I found myself crouching in the shadows, clenching my teeth to still their relentless chatter. A sickly cloying dread hung in the air.

Someone told me that Gloucester had Lord Rivers and Grey beheaded that June. I felt I had no friends left. All my father's trusted cohorts were gone, and I was alone, except for my younger brother Richard. I prayed a great deal because I was afraid that something would happen to my brother and myself. There was a new constable of the Tower, Sir Robert Brackenbury, and strange men became our guard. Then I heard that we were deemed illegitimate. Father had married another woman before Mother, and I wasn't to be King. Guess who was: Richard, Duke of Gloucester. And his son would be Prince of Wales! On July 6, he was crowned King Richard III, only seventy-seven days after Father died.

One night I woke up in my cold dank room in the Tower. I thought I had heard the sound of footsteps and shook my brother. He turned over restlessly.

"Richard," I hissed. "Wake up. Someone's coming."

"Edward, it's the middle of night. Go to sleep."

"No, I hear something."

"It's just a dream."

"You're wrong. I hear footsteps. Maybe it's Gloucester."

Richard yawned. "That would be good. He's quite nice you know."

"He's too busy being King to pay attention to us. Everyone has forgotten about us here in the Tower." Something startled me; I knew I heard something. "Don't you hear that noise?" The silence was heavy, ominous, as the stillness you got in church. Then I heard footsteps coming closer.

My brother and I entered the Tower of London in 1483, and we never came out again. The only thing left of us is two small sobbing ghosts, wearing nightgowns. People reach out for us, but we fade back into the walls where our bodies were concealed.

It wasn't until 1674, when King Charles II ordered the area around the White Tower cleared of all nearby buildings, that our bodies were found in a wooden chest buried at the bottom of a private staircase used to reach a doorway into the Chapel of St. John the Evangelist in the second story of the White Tower. Of course, not everyone is sure that those are our bones and no one is sure about who murdered us. The usual explanation is that two men used our pillows and bedclothes to smother us. We were then walled into a small room to be forgotten for centuries.

**Directions:** Take the Underground to Tower Hill and follow the signs. Once you have passed through the security checks, wait for the next tour by a Yeoman Warder. They do a wonderful job of making the Tower come alive.

# Off With That Head

*Certainly, many executions took place in medieval London before the Tudors, but they were the ones who found the ax a good way to dispose of would-be contenders for the throne.*

*Some were more successful than others in outwitting the executioner. Take Margaret of Salisbury. In many ways, she was another pawn on that chessboard controlled by Kings and their advisers, but she managed to make it to a good old age.*

*Now she too wanders the Tower of London.*

Of Plantagenet stock and members of the House of York, Margaret and her brother Edward had already lost their mother when their father, George, the Duke of Clarence, was killed. Supposedly, Edward IV, his brother. and one of her uncles had him drowned in a butt of malmsey wine (remember Shakespeare's play "Richard III"?). Edward redeemed himself somewhat by permitting the two orphans to be brought up with his children. But what nightmares they must have had. By the time Margaret was twelve, two of Edward's children, Edward V and Richard Duke of York (the famous Little Princes) had disappeared in the Tower; Richard III had reigned and died at the Battle of Bosworth; and Henry VII, the only surviving male representative of the house of Lancaster and the first in the line of the Tudors, had ascended to the throne. In modern terms, we would call this family dysfunctional.

Once the Tudors were in power, they did their best to eradicate the remaining members of the House of York. Royal personages aren't different from anyone else. They just have more to protect. The Tudor colors of white and green along with Tudor arms and the red and white rose appeared everywhere. It was those other nobles who also had royal blood and numerous connections by descent or marriage who were of concern.

The jockeying for power often resulted in conflict, bloodshed and imprisonment - or worse. Margaret's 24-year-old brother, Edward, Earl of Warwick, the last male representative of the Plantagenets, lost his head. By the time she was a young woman, Margaret had lost her mother, father, brother and numerous cousins, aunts and uncles.

Luckily for her, Henry VII arranged for her to marry Sir Richard Pole, when she was about eighteen years old. A Knight of the Garter, he held responsible positions, including Governor to Arthur, the Prince of Wales. The couple appeared to be quite happy, but then he died, leaving her with five children. Once again, she was alone.

When Henry VIII ascended the throne in 1509, he was a glowing representative of the Renaissance. His sparkling court attracted many great scholars, artists and musicians to the new Tudor dynasty. His court had a royal magnificence that fostered loyalty to the throne. The King bought Italian furniture, cloth of gold and damask, had palaces and chapels built, popularized learning and made his court the center of activity. Henry restored the title of Countess of Salisbury, which had been previously held in her family. This move in 1512 brought Margaret good income from her ancestral domains, eventually making her one of the wealthiest peers in England.

Her happiness continued. A devout Roman Catholic, Margaret served Henry's first Queen, Catherine of Aragon, was Princess Mary's sponsor in baptism and acted in the capacity of her mother. In 1516, she was appointed governess to Princess Mary, a high honor indeed.

These were the good years. Her children shared in Margaret's good fortune. She acquired gowns, furs, jewels, and cupboards filled with rich gold plate. Her eldest son, Henry, was created Baron Montague and received large estates. Her son Arthur accompanied Mary Tudor, the King's beloved younger sister, to France for her marriage to King Louis

XII. Her youngest son Geoffrey, like his two older brothers, married an heiress. Her son Reginald was a future Cardinal and the last Catholic Archbishop of Canterbury. After the death of Cardinal Wolsey, Henry VIII contemplated making him Archbishop of York. Catherine of Aragon had happy ideas of bringing a match between him, the handsome son of her longtime friend, and her daughter Princess Mary. Especially gifted, he had great mental abilities, personal beauty and a strong moral code. Unfortunately, the best laid plans of Queens and countesses often go awry.

As countess of Salisbury, Mary was one of the wealthiest English peers. She enjoyed Henry VIII's favor and was a friend of Queen Catherine. Then her daughter, Ursula, married Henry, Lord Stafford, whose father was Lord Stafford, Duke of Buckingham. The Duke could claim royal blood on both the male and female line and saw himself as heir to the kingdom, especially since Henry VIII only had one daughter, Princess Mary, and no sign of any more. The two men were in competition. Henry VIII envied Buckingham because of his wealth, land and royal bloodlines. Like many nobles, Buckingham resented Thomas Wolsey, Henry VIII's advisor, and his influence with the King. Wolsey seized upon Henry's envy and had Buckingham tried for treason. Goodbye Stafford. All his land and estates now belonged to the Crown. Kings do know how to get rich.

Margaret's kinship with Buckingham meant that now she and Princess Mary were separated for four years. Several years passed before the Pole family was restored to favor. Never again would they be as confident of Henry VIII's affection for them.

Henry's romantic inclinations changed the course of history. When Catherine failed to bear him a living son and Anne Boleyn became an "item," Henry requested that the Pope annul his marriage. Ultimately, Parliament passed the Act of Supremacy, which declared the King to be the Supreme Head of the Church of England and denied the authority of the Pope.

Those who did not acknowledge the issue of Henry and Anne as legitimate heirs to the throne and the King as Supreme Head of the Church of England found their heads at risk. The King proclaimed that they would be charged with high treason and punished accordingly. Respected leaders, such as John Fisher, Bishop of Rochester, and Sir Thomas More, once Chancellor of England and a close royal friend, were beheaded for high treason in 1535.

Margaret was not only Catherine's friend and Mary's devoted governess, but she was a good Roman Catholic. Throughout her life, she remained true to her principles and the people she cared about. When she opposed Henry's marriage to Anne, the King exiled her from court. King Henry VIII was not accustomed to opposition. When Margaret's son Reginald didn't support Henry's divorce, he left for self-imposed exile in France and Italy in 1532. There, safe in Europe, he denounced Henry's policies in an uncompromising document and denied Henry's Act of Supremacy.

Unfortunately, his mother and other family members were still within Henry's reach. He had two of her sons and other relatives arrested on a charge of treason, though Cromwell had previously written that they had "little offended save that he [the Cardinal] is of their kin." Committed to the Tower, they, with the exception of Geoffrey Pole, were executed. Margaret was imprisoned in the Tower, where she suffered from the severity of the weather and the lack of appropriate clothing. Probably, Henry thought that Cardinal Pole would surrender himself to save his almost seventy-year-old mother, but the Cardinal kept his head and remained in Europe.

Consequently, Henry's vengeance now fell on his mother, Margaret, who was sentenced to be executed on May 27, 1541. The old woman refused to lay her head on the block, so the inexperienced executioner was forced to swing at her as she struggled. At one point, she leapt from the block and was chased by the executioner, who must have been panicked though not as panicked as Margaret must have been. Although Margaret was small and frail, the young man flailed away at her head and neck, hacking her to pieces for some time before she died. Not that death by ax is ever easy, but her death was particularly gruesome according to all reports.

The ax was a great way to dispose of would-be contenders for the throne. *Courtesy of D. Peter Lund*

Her body was interred in the Chapel of St. Peter ad Vincula in the Tower. Everything she had worked so hard to achieve was gone: her many residences, her lands, and her titles. Her eldest son was executed as a traitor, another had attempted suicide, and third was living in exile. In 1886, 354 years later, Pope Leo XIII beatified her as Blessed Margaret Pole.

The countess's ghost is one of many that haunt the Tower of London. It is said that every year, on the anniversary of the execution, her ghost can be seen and heard re-enacting the terrible scene on Tower Green.

**Directions:** Take the Underground to Tower Hill and follow the signs.

# The Charterhouse

*London has many medieval streets, picturesque courtyards, and ancient buildings. Some of the more ancient buildings in London have several ghosts. Often a lone monk from the sixteenth century wanders about the ancient courtyard of the Charterhouse. Some evenings, a headless ghost, a former duke, joins him. These ghosts are not just aimless spirits meandering about. They have definite roles in history, and perhaps they believe their business on earth is not done.*

The Black Death reached the shores of England in the summer of 1348. The overcrowding and primitive sanitation of the cities aided its spread. On November 1, the plague reached London, and almost forty percent of the population fell victim to the pestilence. In 1349, First Baron Walter de Manny, a soldier of fortune, bought land near Smithfield, London. Some of the land was consecrated and used to inter large numbers of the Black Death victims.

For medieval Christians, one of the worst aspects of the plague was that its victims died without having a chance to confess their sins. To remedy this situation, a Carthusian monastery called Charterhouse was built outside the burial pit. Here, the monks prayed for those who died from the 1348 Black Death. Mass was not only for the living congregation but for the dead in search of eternal peace.

In the early fifteenth century, religion was a dominant force. Life was a mixture of symbol and ritual, ringing bells and wafting incense, washing of feet on Maundy Thursday and creeping to the cross on Good Friday. The devout English attended mass faithfully. The church profited from all this and was by far the largest landowner in England.

Charterhouse flourished. Known for their devout rendition of the Liturgy of the Hours, the Carthusian monks were much sought after for their spiritual counsel and prayers. Many people came to them for spiritual rejuvenation, including Thomas More. The monks each had their own small building and garden of herbs such as parsley, fennel, sage, mint and rue. There were beds of onions, leeks, pumpkins, shallots and cucumber.

There were no ghosts then.

In 1527,when Henry VIII decided to divorce the aging Catherine of Aragon, Rome refused to annul the marriage. This action set off a chain of events, which resulted in Henry becoming the Supreme Head of the Church of England. Concurrently, a strong minority in England and on the continent was challenging the central role of the priest and the Roman Catholic Church. Perhaps, they wondered, every man could have his own spiritual relationship with God. Maybe the church had fallen from the pursuit of Christian perfection. Had the religious houses become business corporations with their great estates? The flaunted wealth of the religious institutions certainly attracted envy, particularly from a King who needed to pay his bills.

The timing of the Reformation was perfect for Henry VIII who wanted to divorce Catherine of Aragon so he could marry Anne Boleyn and father a male heir. In 1535, Henry VIII's chief minister, Thomas Cromwell, sent out inspectors to the approximately eight hundred monasteries and convents in England. Amazingly, the inspectors found evidence that these religious institutions were corrupt, but then Cromwell and their King would have been most unhappy if they hadn't. The empty royal coffers and English courtiers immediately benefited from one of the largest land grabs in the history of England.

## St. John Houghton

In 1531, John Houghton was elected Prior of the Charterhouse. That was unfortunate for Houghton because it was not a good time to be a prior. Tired of waiting for the Pope to annul his marriage to Catherine of Aragon, Henry VIII

Often, a lone monk from the sixteenth century wanders about the ancient courtyard of the Charterhouse. Some evenings, a headless ghost—a former duke—joins him. *Courtesy of D. Peter Lund*

had taken matters into his own hand. In 1534, Parliament passed the Act of Succession, vesting the succession of the English Crown in his children with Anne Boleyn and making Henry "the only supreme head of the Church in England." Encouraged by Cromwell, Henry sent royal commissioners out to secure the taking of the oath. When Houghton and a friar refused to sign, they were taken to the Tower of London. Ultimately, they decided that they could sign by adding the clause "in so far as the law of God permits."

A year later under the 1534 Act of Supremacy, Henry VIII required that everyone swear an oath renouncing the Pope's authority and recognizing the King as the supreme head of the Church in England – without any additional clauses. Anyone who refused to swear this oath would be charged with treason. Almost everyone swore, but Houghton and two priors from other monasteries would not. They were arrested, called before a special commission, which sentenced them to be hanged, drawn and quartered at Tyburn on May 4, 1535.

From his prison cell in the Tower, Thomas More saw the three Carthusian priors being taken to Tyburn. Supposedly, he said to his daughter: "Look, Meg, these blessed fathers be now as cheerfully going to their deaths as bridegrooms to their marriage!" A year later, More went to the block as traitor to King Henry VIII and a martyr of the Roman Catholic Church.

Henry VIII's men nailed the arm of the prior to these gates. *Courtesy of D. Peter Lund*

After Houghton was hung, he was taken down alive to be quartered. According to the story, as the executioner tore open his chest to remove his heart before quartering him, Houghton prayed, "O Jesu, what wouldst thou do with my heart?" After his death, his body was chopped to pieces and hung in different parts of London. To persuade the surviving monks to sign the oath, the King's soldiers nailed one of Houghton's arms onto the gates of Charterhouse.

Not even the sight of their prior's arm on the Charterhouse gates could make the monks swear the oath. Instead, they prayed for the strength to remain true to their faith. Supposedly, one night as they prayed, a bolt of heavenly flame caused their candles to ignite into brilliant flames. Unfortunately, Houghton's spirit could not help them resist the King: ten monks were taken to the nearby Newgate Prison; nine of these men starved to death and the tenth was executed at Tower Hill. Other monks were executed. Together with Houghton, they constitute the group known as the Carthusian Martyrs. John Houghton was canonized, but sainthood hasn't stopped his ghost from praying for those who died from the 1348 Black Death as he wanders the cobbled streets around Charterhouse Square in the quiet of the night.

The remaining monks turned over what was left of Charterhouse to the King and his cronies. By 1540, all of the English monasteries and nunneries were empty, and the buildings sold to the up-and-coming nobility.

**Thomas Howard, Fourth Duke of Norfolk**

One such nobleman was Thomas Howard, Duke of Norfolk and the first Earl of Southampton. In the early years of Elizabeth's reign, the fourth Duke of Norfolk, a cousin to the Queen, was a powerful magnate. Thanks to his three advantageous marriages, he was the wealthiest landowner in the country. He professed to be Protestant but had Catholic leanings. He had inherited the dukedom of Norfolk, become a Knight of the Garter in April 1559, and played a role in the English campaign in Scotland in that year. In January 1566, Charles IX of France dubbed him and Robert Dudley, the Earl of Leicester, Knights of St. Michael, as the two foremost English nobles.

But Norfolk, like others before him, made a bad decision. He became involved with Mary, Queen of Scots. In 1568, Norfolk participated in a commission that inquired into Scottish affairs after the flight of Mary, Queen of Scots to England. A widower, he conducted secret negotiations to marry Mary, who had fled to England. When Elizabeth heard of the proposed marriage from the women of the court, she forgave Norfolk for scheming to marry Mary but forbid any marriage.

Leaving court without the Queen's leave–a rash act–Norfolk ran to his country estate. That act alone made him appear guilty. Summoned back, he was sent to the Tower while the Northern nobles of "the old religion" rose in rebellion. He was released, but then he became involved in the Ridolfi plot, which involved English Catholics rebelling, a Spanish army invading, marrying Mary Queen of Scots and assassinating Elizabeth. The plot failed, and Norfolk and others were arrested for treason.

Tried on January 6, 1572, Norfolk was found guilty and sentenced to death. For several months, Elizabeth held out against executing him – after all he was a relative through her mother. But enough was enough. On June 2, 1572, the fourth Duke of Norfolk, who had made a foolish choice, went to the scaffold on Tower Hill.

After his death, the main staircase of the Charterhouse became haunted. People report seeing Howard's ghost coming down the staircase holding his missing head under his arm. Today, Houghton and Norfolk prowl the halls of Charterhouse and the nearby alleys. They each made a decision that led to a violent end. Their decision affected others. Perhaps this haunts them.

**Directions:** The London Charterhouse became a hospice for elderly male residents. Today some twenty or so elderly men live amid the ancient courts and the prowling ghosts of this wonderful old mansion. It may be visited by guided tour only. The southern side is open to view from Charterhouse Square. The nearest tube is Barbican but Farringdon tube and surface rail station are also close.

# My Ghosts

*These bloody days have broken my heart;*
*My lust, my youth did then depart,*
*And blind desire of estate;*
*Who haste's to climb seeks to revert:*
*Of truth, circa Regna tonat (it thunders around the throne).*
Thomas Wyatt on the occasion of Anne's imprisonment.

**Henry VIII's Family**

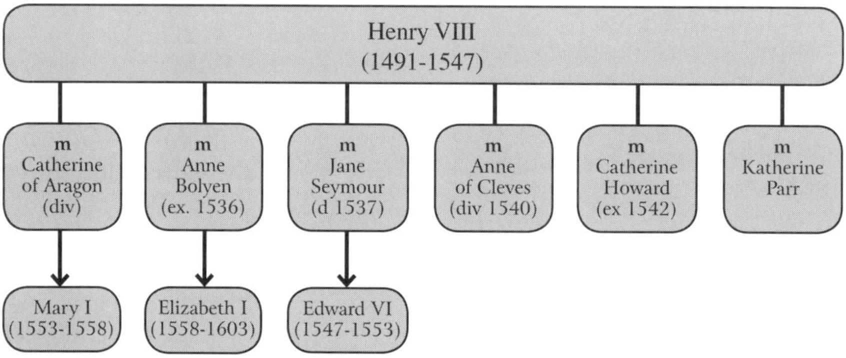


My ghosts do not care whether it is dark or light. They come and go as they wish. Waking or sleeping makes no difference to them. I just sit in my chair staring out at the greenness of the land, and George appears. His smile looks beyond me—as if he is looking at something in the distance. The light, whether it is moon or sun, shines through him. When he is gone, the dust motes dance in his place, and I cry and cry.

Anne never rests, but she was always the most intense of the three children who survived childhood. She wanders the Tower of London. Her headless body arrives in a phantom coach at Blickling Hall, her childhood home. On the anniversary of her execution, some say she wanders through the grounds and attics of Rochford Hall. Of course, people always talk about my daughter Anne. She was Queen after all, and her daughter was one of the best rulers England ever had. But I lost two children that week in May – two children born of my loins – two vital passionate children and now they haunt the Tower and me. People say that Anne's ghost returns frequently to the Queen's House at the Tower. People don't talk about George – perhaps because he was only a Viscount – not someone as important as a Queen. But George was such a love, and mothers and sons do have a special bond.

But let's start at the beginning. I am Lady Elizabeth Howard born in Arundel Castle in Sussex. I am the daughter of Thomas Howard, second Duke of Norfolk, and Elizabeth Tilney, a direct descendant of Edward I of England. My family had supported Richard III so we had been away from court for a while. When I was younger, I was lady-in-waiting to Elizabeth of York, the daughter of Edward IV and older sister to the Little Princes who disappeared.

Brought up to obey my parents and to defer to their opinion – as I would later defer to my husband's – I married Thomas Boleyn at age thirteen in 1499. We moved to his family home at Blickling Castle in Norfolk. Born in 1477, Thomas entered into royal service early. He fought for Henry VII and escorted Princess Margaret to Scotland where she would marry James IV. In 1509, when King Henry VIII was crowned King of England, Thomas was knighted. In the next several years, my three beautiful babies were born: Mary, George and Anne. In 1505, we moved to Hever Castle, which my husband had inherited.

The blond brick walled house with its decorative chimneys and water lily studded moat rested in the grassy meadows at the fork of the gentle River Eden. The oldest part of the castle is a gatehouse and a walled bailey, dating back to 1270. We added a Tudor dwelling within the walls and settled into that lovely Kent countryside with its yew-lined lanes, grassy swards, and the drone of bees in the beds of roses and Sweet William. Great forests surrounded us with game, grain-filled meadows, and wide marshes thick with birds.

We were so happy there. We had a marriage where we really cared for each other. Thomas would look at me, and I would feel a frisson of delight crawl up my spine. A look from him, the press of his hand on my flesh, his lip against my ear overwhelmed me. When he held me close in his arms, I felt warm, safe and happy. Not only did we love each other, but we had three wonderful children.

We planted a flower garden with foxglove, Sweet William, yellow and orange lilies, and, of course, my all-essential herb garden. The years passed, and life was good. Each night I would read to the children; then they would go to bed, and Thomas and I would have our own time. He still made me feel on fire with the way he brushed my hair back from my face and touched my skin with such sureness. He would put his arms around me, and I could hardly breathe for I loved him so much.

I worked hard to educate the children. George was very bright. I don't even have to close my eyes to conjure up the memory of him, fragrant and damp from a swim in the lake, radiating heat as his little breaths grew slower and slower the closer he got to sleep. Anne was good at art, music and languages. I also taught her religion, as well as embroidery, reading and writing. My daughter Mary was beautiful in the expected blond, blue-eyed way. But Anne, with her masses of lustrous dark hair, mischievous black eyes, long, slender neck and regal bearing, had a "way" about her that attracted attention. She was clever, coquettish, strong-willed, and she knew how to get her own way. Anne's French governess would shake her head admiringly. "She is very clever, your Anne. She will go far." I smiled happily. I told Thomas she had inherited his gift with languages. He would smile proudly. Between the two of them, we might return to court.

And perhaps that's where things went wrong. Thomas did have a gift for languages, including Latin, which made him a good diplomat. One of his first missions was to meet with Margaret of Austria, regent of the Netherlands for Charles V, to deal with the planned invasion of France. He was also the English ambassador in France from 1519 to 1520 and involved in the arrangement of the Field of Cloth of Gold. A trusted adviser, he also accompanied Henry VIII to his meeting with Charles V at Gravelines.

Our first major disagreement came after Thomas's appointment as Ambassador to the Court of Margaret of Savoy, Archduchess of Austria and Regent of the Netherlands in 1512. He wanted to send our girls abroad to further their education. "Listen wife," his voice had an unfamiliar edge of authority. "I see a golden opportunity for our lovely dark-eyed Anne and sweet Mary at the Savoy court. I am going to send them so they can take advantage of a free and elegant finishing school."

"No, Thomas. They're too young. They're learning all about courtly behavior here. They're learning how to dance, sing..."

"They need to learn how to behave in courtly society and to make useful social contacts. I have great plans for all three children. Believe me, the opportunity is fortuitous."

"Oh, no, Thomas. We need to protect them – their chastity, their reputations."

"We cannot forego this opportunity for advancement," I shook my head. He continued, "This is a wonderful chance, my dear, and at no cost to us."

"You're always thinking of money, Thomas. They are just children. Our children." I wasn't sure that I wanted them in that role at all. Mary didn't always use her head. Easily persuaded, she could run into trouble. Anne had a sharp way about her that needed to be mellowed.

"Elizabeth, imagine it. It is the highest rung of the ladder for now. Once they are educated there, they can return and be one of Queen Catherine's ladies." We compromised, and only Anne went.

A year later, Thomas announced that our Mary had been appointed Maid of Honor to Henry VIII's sister Mary, when she was to wed the aged King Louis XII of France. I was unable to gainsay my obdurate husband. I had lost one child to his ambition, I thought to myself. I still had Anne and George.

Not for long though. Anne joined her sister Mary at the French court, where both were attendants to the eighteen-year-old Queen Mary. In January 1515, King Louis XII died, leaving Mary a widow, but she married Charles Brandon, Duke of Suffolk, in secret and left France in disgrace. Quick on his feet as always, Thomas established my girls in the household of Queen Claude of France. Given Mary's lovely looks and easygoing personality, King Francois I soon noticed her. In later years, he referred to her as "my English mare." Not very flattering! Even worse, she was considered as a "very great wanton with a most infamous reputation." Meanwhile, George was learning how to be a courtier. He had been a page at court and played a part in the 1514-1515 Christmas revels.

After The Field of the Cloth of Gold in June of 1520, which was a chance for the nobility to preen their feathers, Mary came home. Although the meeting between Francois I of France and Henry VIII accomplished little, it proved a victory for my husband: Henry VIII had noticed Mary when he visited our manor. She became lady-in-waiting to Catherine of Aragon and mistress of the King. My beloved husband profited from her liaison, receiving honors and stewardships. He was awarded possessions from the estate of the executed Duke of Buckingham and became Treasurer of the Household,

Ambassador to Spain, Knight of the Garter and Clerk of the King's Jewels.

Mary married a wealthy and well-connected courtier in 1520. When Mary had a child in 1526, whom she named Henry, which was rumored to be the King's, Henry's interest faded. The same year, my wonderful son George was married to Jane Parker. Thomas said, "It's a favorable marital alliance that will enhance our family's honor and prestige."

"But dear, Jane strikes me as so conniving."

Thomas ignored my comment. "It might even facilitate the development of some beneficial personal and business allegiances for us." And so their marriage occurred. They never seemed to be very happy together. Instead, George spent most of his time with the courtiers at court. He and Anne were quite close.

In 1522, Anne came to the English court after many years at the glittering French court. She had charm, style, wit and a will that provoked male interest – too much – so she left for a while but returned in 1526 as a maid of honor to the Queen. Mary had already earned our family many favors. Wanting to keep a good thing going, Thomas suggested to Anne that she catch Henry's eye. It would be important for the family, he told us. Hah! What more did we need? But I didn't protest because I was the obedient wife. He was the head of the family, I told myself. When I married him, I entered another family, and I was his dearly beloved but subordinate partner. I could disagree, but he would decide.

Anne had learned her lessons in France exceedingly well. Her great dark eyes shone with her wit and intelligence. She could sing, dance and speak French fluently. Her vitality and interest in philosophy and politics made her the center of attention in any gathering. Although she was about sixteen years younger than the King, she captivated the thirty-six year-old Henry. He was smitten, and Thomas was thrilled.

“Did you see him kiss her,” Thomas would hiss at me. “That kiss is her destiny – and our fortune, Elizabeth.”

I was appalled. Anne’s independence and her drive would lead to trouble, I thought. Nothing good could come from this, but my beloved husband was encouraging her in his desire to win yet more power and influence. Fortunately, Anne had seen what had happened to Mary so she insisted that she would only give herself to the King when she was his Queen. How could this occur, she would say with a toss of her shiny dark hair, when he was already married to Catherine – who couldn’t bear him a male heir? Then she would laugh and laugh, with her dark eyes sparkling. Everyone knew that Henry wanted a son and that Catherine was approaching the age where she could no longer bear children. If she held out for marriage, Anne could become Queen and the mother of the prince and heir Henry so fervently desired.

And so Anne said “No,” which only made the King, who was accustomed to getting what he wanted, more determined. Anne presented him with a challenge.

“I tell you, Elizabeth,” said Thomas one night, “Watching this is like watching a fire. It started with only a few small sparks, but now it is burning faster and higher – so much so that it just can’t go out on its own.”

“Which terrifies me. The King is a determined man. Catherine won’t let him annul her marriage, and where will that leave our Anne?”

“Anne has received many expensive gifts from the King. The French King is supportive, and I believe Henry will authorize his new minister Thomas Cromwell to implement procedures that will allow Anne to be Queen.”

I put down my embroidery, held out my arms to Thomas and said, “If that’s so, let’s go to bed now, dear, and appreciate our blessings on this cold March night.”

"Certainly. Trust me, my dear. It will be a good marriage." He smiled, smoothed back my hair, and stood up, grasping my hand. "Now about that wonderful idea of yours."

But there weren't many more wonderful "ideas" like that. I disliked what Thomas was doing to Anne and Mary. He was pushing them too hard. They were forgetting the lessons I had taught them as children about being kind and gentle and thinking of others. George was the King's cupbearer and Gentleman of the Privy Chamber. In 1528, he became Esquire of the Body with an annuity of 50 marks and Master of the Buckhounds and was knighted the next year.

Of course, Thomas profited throughout. In June 1525, he was elevated to peerage as Viscount Rochford. In 1529, he was made the Earl of Wiltshire and received the Earldom of Ormonde. One of Henry's major advisers, he also met with Charles V, François I and Pope Clement VII concerning the annulment. While I was frightened by what the future might hold, he wanted the honors that came to him from Henry dallying with our daughter Mary and then marrying Anne. As much as I loved Thomas, I felt as if he was using Anne and her startling looks as one uses a harlot. But I didn't have the courage to stand up to Thomas. I let it all happen. My mother taught me that as a woman I was to listen and to be agreeable. "Since God told that sinner Eve that Adam should rule over her, we need to accept your father's and then your husband's approval as the proper standard for your behavior."

The King courted Anne for six years. After years of fruitless negotiations and high drama, Anne and Henry married in secret, his marriage to Catherine was annulled, and Anne became pregnant. In June 1533, she achieved her dream: she became Henry's Queen and the Queen of England. Her coronation was quite splendid, but the English people loved Catherine and hated Anne, calling her "witch" and "the concubine."

We had more estates, stewardships, jewels and goods than we would ever need as Thomas continued the struggle to preserve and advance our lineage. We rarely saw each other now. I remained in Anne's household throughout her time as Queen consort. My wonderful son George was her lieutenant in the Privy Chamber, and poor Mary, who lived an impoverished life in the country, was practically ignored.

Henry married Anne when she was about five months pregnant. On September 7, 1533, Anne gave birth–not to the anticipated male heir but to Elizabeth. Anne suffered a miscarriage in 1534. Never popular with the people, and testing Henry's patience with her failure to produce a male heir, Anne behaved arrogantly and grew to be hated at court.

On the other hand, Anne was a good religious example and had a major role in dispensing charity. Certainly, she furthered the careers of many of her relatives but she also supported those who supported the royal supremacy and favored scriptural translations. She just couldn't present the King with that desired male heir.

In the next several years, Henry VIII was declared the Supreme Head of the Church of England, which made him the head of the Church of England as well as the King of England. Under the Act of Succession, only the children resulting from his marriage to Anne would be lawful heirs. People were asked to swear allegiance. Most did, but some powerful magnates such as Sir Thomas More and Bishop Fisher of Rochester didn't, which led to their execution. Anne was hated even more.

Catherine died and Anne delivered a stillborn son in January of 1536, losing her last chance to preserve her marriage. The King began to pay attention to gentle Jane Seymour–a far cry from my passionate, assertive daughter. Furious and scared, Anne stormed about, accusing, shouting and crying. She danced, sang and made caustic remarks

The Tower of London, a complex of many buildings set within two concentric rings of defensive walls and a moat, is a famous and centuries-old prison.
*Courtesy of D. Peter Lund*

about the King's prowess in the royal bed and his poetry. Her ambition was her downfall, and she dragged my only son George with her.

Henry VIII was no longer listening, and Anne had made her enemies–one being Cromwell. Mark Smeaton, her musician, was arrested and tortured, and the "confession" began to be heard. Anne's flirtatious ways and playful glances were considered evidence of actual infidelity. She and her alleged lovers, including my son George, were arrested on the grounds of multiple adultery and taken to the Tower of London. The Church regarded adultery as a sin and treated it as a crime to be punished.

My husband was no help. He denounced the crimes of all of those accused. He tried Mark Smeaton, Sir Francis Weston, William Brereton and Sir Henry Norris for alleged adultery with Anne and found them guilty–although we all

The circular memorial commemorates the ten executions that have taken place on Tower Green, within the Tower's walls. The arches supporting the upper glass disk are engraved with the names of the executed; a poem written by the sculptor encircles the memorial. *Courtesy of D. Peter Lund*

knew that the charges were trumped up. King Henry excused Thomas from the task of condemning his own children to death for treason, adultery and incest. I wonder if he would have been able to.

I was helpless. My George was in trouble, and I couldn't do anything. How could I lose my strong, faithful son? As for Anne, I always knew that all her passionate intensity could only lead to disaster. And how could I love my husband Thomas when he had turned his back on our children and put his fortune first?

On May 17, my son and the other alleged lovers were executed. Henry VIII agreed to import a French executioner with a French double bladed sword for Anne's execution. On May 19, 1536, my daughter Anne Boleyn was executed on Tower Green. I have heard that she said, "I hear the executioner is very good, and I have a little neck." Then she put her hands around her neck and laughed. When it was over and as the executioner held her head high for the crowd to behold, her mouth continued to pray and her eyes moved as if watching the crowd. Her body and head were buried in an old arrow chest in an unmarked grave in the Chapel of St. Peter ad Vincula. Within 24 hours, Jane Seymour and Henry VIII were formally betrothed. Life goes on, and so do my ghosts. George holds out his arms for me, and Anne cries, "Watch out for my daughter Elizabeth."

Over the years, many tower guards have spotted Anne. One private, who was found unconscious outside the King's House on a winter's night in 1864, was subjected to a court martial. In his hearing, he described how a strange white figure had emerged from the dawn mist. The figure continued to approach him despite his warning. When he ran his rifle bayonet through the body, a flash of fire ran up the barrel and he passed out. Fortunately, several other soldiers who had been in the nearby Bloody Tower told the hearing that they too had seen the ghost. After learning that the incident had occurred just under the room where Anne Boleyn spent the night before her execution, the court-martial judges cleared the sentry.

Sentries have often seen her ghost pacing up and down outside the tiny chapel. One night, one of the guards noticed a light shining from inside the chapel. Peering through a window, he saw ghostly knights and ladies process slowly up the aisle, led by a woman resembling Anne. When she reached the altar, they all vanished, leaving the chapel in darkness again.

**Directions:** Take the Underground to Tower Hill and follow signs.

# Burn Baby Burn

Smithfield has been a site for executions for a long time. About fifty Protestants, dissenters, and other religious reformers—known as the Marian martyrs—were executed here under the reign of Mary I. Coin forgers were boiled in oil here during the sixteenth century.

Ultimately, it became a meat market–such irony. Dickens described it this way:

> *It was market-morning. The ground was covered, nearly ankle-deep, with filth and mire; a thick steam, perpetually rising from the reeking bodies of the cattle, and mingling with the fog, which seemed to rest upon the chimney-tops, hung heavily above. All the pens in the centre of the large area, and as many temporary pens as could be crowded into the vacant space, were filled with sheep; tied up to posts by the gutter side were long lines of beasts and oxen, three or four deep. Countrymen, butchers, drovers, hawkers, boys, thieves, idlers, and vagabonds of every low grade, were mingled together in a mass; the whistling of drovers, the barking dogs, the bellowing and plunging of the oxen, the bleating of sheep, the grunting and squeaking of pigs, the cries of hawkers, the shouts, oaths, and quarrelling on all sides; the ringing of bells and roar of voices, that issued from every public-house; the crowding, pushing, driving, beating, whooping and yelling; the hideous and discordant dim that resounded from every corner of the market; and the unwashed, unshaven, squalid, and dirty figures constantly running to and fro, and bursting in and out of the throng; rendered it a stunning and bewildering scene, which quite confounded the senses.*
>
> Charles Dickens describing Smithfield in *Oliver Twist*

When I went to my first sleepover camp, I heard the scary story of Bloody Mary, the evil spirit who will scratch your eyes out when called. According to the legend, you can summon this evil woman by chanting "Bloody Mary" into a mirror anywhere from three to thirteen times in a darkened room lit only by a candle. Once this spirit has decided that you have chanted the appropriate number of times, the spirit appears in the mirror and claws your eyes out. Death promptly follows. Who Bloody Mary is remains a mystery. Most versions point to a woman named Mary Worth, who was horribly disfigured in a car crash. Some people still tell of a witch who was burned at the stake and returned for revenge, or perhaps it is the devil himself who comes for your soul. Some say that Bloody Mary is the oldest child of Henry VIII, who became Queen in 1553. Others say that she is not the source of the campfire Bloody Mary.

All agree, however, that the Queen known as Bloody Mary is the source of anguished screams around dawn in Smithfield. And if you sniff, you can smell that sickly sweet aroma of burning flesh that is carried by the early morning breeze. Although Mary I of England had a short reign, she left a legacy of death, torture and repression.

When I was a child, I was fascinated by fire: the snap and crackle of the ebbing fire, the shadows cast by candlelight, the hot, fierce flame of a new fire, the glowing embers of a brush fire, the blinding smoke and scent of leaves burning in the fall. I also had a mother who was an aficionado of English history. No Dr. Seuss for me. I learned about the mysterious death of The Little Princes, the sad and short life of Lady Jane Grey, the heartbroken toy spaniel curled up in Mary Queen of Scots' gown after she lost her head. One of my mother's favorite tales was Bloody Mary.

Once upon a time, she would begin, Princess Mary was an adored young princess with red-gold curls who lived in a grand palace with many people who doted on her. Her mother was Catherine of Aragon, and her father was the handsome young Henry VIII. "This girl never cries," Henry would boast as he proudly carried her on his shoulder showing her off to all the courtiers. By the time, she was three years old, she had her own separate household and saw her parents mainly on holidays. Henry arranged several betrothals for his daughter: one with Dauphin Francis, son of the French King Francis, and another with Charles V, the King of Spain and the Holy Roman Emperor. When Mary was nine years old, Henry gave her her own court at Ludlow Castle. "Imagine," my mother would gasp, "She had more than three hundred attendants." Calling her the Princess of Wales, Henry VIII said she was "the greatest pearl in the kingdom." Two years later, he was arranging yet another betrothal for her with King Francis' second son, Henry. Certainly, Mary was a good diplomatic tool.

Then the rumors began. Henry VIII wanted to annul his marriage with Catherine of Aragon and marry the enthralling Anne Boleyn. The Pope didn't agree, and years passed. In 1531, Henry ordered Catherine to leave his court and to never see her daughter again.

Henry VIII was a cruel man.

By annulling his marriage to Catherine, Henry made Mary illegitimate. Mother commented, "A major downfall for the oldest child of the King of a powerful country – especially one who had been 'the greatest pearl.'" Now, she was nothing.

He then married Anne Boleyn and created the Church of England. When Anne had a daughter Elizabeth, she was proclaimed Princess of Wales while Mary was demoted to Lady Mary instead of Princess Mary. What an insult! Refusing to accept her new status, Mary insisted that she was Henry's child born in true matrimony. Henry punished her by eliminating her personal entourage and income and making her a lady-in-waiting to the infant Elizabeth. "A humbling experience," said Mother.

During the next several years, Parliament passed the Act of Succession confirming Mary's illegitimate status and the Oath of Supremacy, stating that the English monarch rather than the Pope was now the ultimate authority on all religious matters. Henry's subjects were required to swear an oath renouncing the Pope's authority and recognizing the King as the supreme head of the new Church of England. Anyone who refused to swear this oath was charged with treason. Few dared to disobey Henry VIII, but those who did, such as his friend and former chancellor, Sir Thomas More, and John Fisher, the bishop of Rochester, were executed. In 1536, Catherine of Aragon died; Henry, tired of Anne Boleyn, had her executed; and he promptly married Jane Seymour.

Mary had always blamed Anne Boleyn for Henry's behavior towards her mother and herself. Although Henry's newest Queen, Jane Seymour, pled her case, Henry refused to reconcile with Mary until she admitted that her parents' marriage was invalid, that she herself was illegitimate, and that the King – not the Pope – was the supreme head of the Church of England. Reluctantly, Mary gave in. She probably hated herself, I thought, for yielding to her father.

"Her only hope was that one day she would be Queen," said my mother. " Perhaps one day she could bring England back to the Roman Catholic Church. Her mother was dead; her beloved governess, Margaret, Countess of Salisbury, gone; her father was destroying the Catholic monasteries and nunneries throughout England and had a third wife; and she had no marriage prospects. Life did not treat Mary well," said my mother. "She probably saw little hope – but she had her faith."

In 1537, Jane Seymour, Henry's third wife, succeeded in presenting Henry with a healthy son, Edward VI. She died soon after.

**Edward VI**

Three stepmothers later, Edward VI, a great adherent of the reformed faith, ascended the throne at age nine. Like his half-sisters Elizabeth and Mary, he had received the best humanist education available at that time. Edward's entire rule was mediated through a regency council, as he never reached maturity. During his reign, England established a Protestant form of worship. The changes ranged from removing the statues of the Virgin Mary and the candles from churches to permitting clergy to marry to conducting all rites in English. Thomas Cranmer, Archbishop of Canterbury, who had been instrumental in publishing the Bible, helped complete the English Book of Common Prayer. Now that the citizens could read these two works in English, their religious and spiritual lives changed. It was the time of the Reformation, and many citizens happily accepted Protestantism and the absence of a papal interference in English affairs.

Almost thirty-one years old, Mary openly held Latin Mass in her private chapels, defying the law that required all clergy to use the new prayer book and communion rites. "Take away my life," she said, "rather than the old religion." She demonstrated her defiance by riding to Westminister with each servant wearing a forbidden rosary.

Because of Mary's bias for the Roman Catholic Church, Edward, a strong adherent of the Reformed faith, left the crown to the Protestant Lady Jane Grey when he died at age fifteen of tuberculosis. But Jane was deposed within nine days, and the people were delighted when Mary assumed the throne in 1553 (see "The Pawn"). She was thirty-seven and unmarried. If Mother's story had stopped there with everyone living happily ever after, it would have been an ok story, except for poor Lady Jane Grey and her husband.

### Mary I

But the story didn't stop there. The Queen needed a Catholic heir, so Mary insisted on marrying Philip of Spain, much to the horror of the English who detested the Spanish. Two months later, she announced her pregnancy. Once again,

England would have a Catholic King. Mary seized upon the opportunity to bring the country back to the Roman Catholic Church with its papal authority and away from what she called heresy. Out of hiding came the statues and the vestments; once again, people listened to Latin in church. Parliament repealed the Act of Supremacy, reestablished papal supremacy and revived the laws for heresy.

Mary had Archbishop Cranmer burned at the stake for his heresy and replaced him with Cardinal Reginald Pole, the son of her governess, the Countess of Salisbury. He concentrated on trying to restore the church to its pre-Reformation state. The bishops were given permission to investigate suspected heresy and to hand over those found guilty to secular authorities for burning at the stake. The property of a convicted heretic automatically reverted to the Crown. "Nothing like a nice fire to make royalty rich!" pointed out Mother.

In January of 1555, the burnings throughout the country in public places like Smithfield began. Imagine what life must have been like. I could almost smell the fires, hear the crackle of the logs and see the horror in the victims' eyes. I wondered what it would be like to know that you were doing things that could have you burned at the stake? Would I, who cried when I bumped my knee, be able to withstand such pain?

Although other Tudor monarchs had persecuted and executed those they considered heretics, Mary launched an unparalleled reign of terror in England. But it backfired. People associated the burnings with the Pope and the Spaniards and toughened their commitment to the Reformed faith. Over the next several years—approximately 300 men and women—died at the stake.

Mother said that according to Mary, heretics deserved to die. She wanted them to suffer a taste of hellfire on earth so that they would repent at their end. She also considered it her duty to punish those who had sinned against God and his laws. She

During the reign of Mary I, religious reformers, Protestants, and other dissenters were persecuted and burned at the stake for their beliefs.
*Courtesy of D. Peter Lund*

emphasized that green wood should not be used, since its smoke was likely to suffocate the victims before they suffered the full agony of the flames. Sounded rather vengeful to me.

Frequently, the executions were mismanaged. One victim burned for almost an hour because the gunpowder bag hanging around his neck did not explode. He begged the crowd to fan the flames in order to end his agony. A pregnant woman gave birth as she was burning. But the baby was cast back into the flames. Queen Mary did not permit the officials to be merciful. She admonished one sheriff who reprieved a heretic who had recanted as the fire was lit.

Those who didn't hold with Mary Tudor's religious opinions quickly found their way to the stake. Numerous Protestant leaders were executed in the Marian persecutions. Others chose exile, and around 800 people left the country. "You have to wonder," Mother mused, "Was she getting her revenge on her father who had annulled his marriage with

At Smithfield, the condemned were tied to the stake so that they looked to the east and to St. Bart's great church door (see "Rahere's Sandals"). In 1849, workmen found a number of stones, blackened with fire, ashes, charred human bones, and charred oak posts. A staple and a ring were fastened to one post. *Courtesy of D. Peter Lund*

her mother, making her a bastard, and destroyed the Catholic faith in England. Was this payback for the time she had to yield to Princess Elizabeth? She had two Protestant siblings, but she was in control now."

The Marian persecutions, particularly as recorded in Foxe's *Book of Martyrs* (1563), led to her nickname, Bloody Mary.

Although the Protestant leadership was destroyed, their martyrdom strengthened the resolve of the citizens, who affirmed their beliefs. Farmers and weavers, housewives and teachers chose to die in the flames rather than renounce their faith. Stories were told of those who prayed for their executioners and who sang hymns as the flames consumed them.

"Fortunately," Mother commented wryly, "Mary only reigned for five years. When she died, people joyfully celebrated the ascension of Elizabeth I, a Protestant. She swiftly stopped the burnings, and by 1559 Protestantism had become England's state religion. Queen Elizabeth was the head of the English church, and Cranmer's prayer book was used for all religious services. To this day, a British monarch has to be Protestant to ascend the throne. The fires of Smithfield resulted in a Protestant nation."

**Directions:** From Barbican station, turn right as soon as you exit the station and immediately right again into Long Lane. Then walk along this road, into West Smithfield with the market on the right. Visit the small park in the center.

# The Pawn

I can hear them hammering nails into the scaffold. Soon they will come for me, and I will be no more. Once life was so glorious, but then it all fell apart.

My wife once told me that her grandmother believed that we are all pawns on a great chessboard, and the major moves in our lives happen without our knowledge or even agreement. Her grandmother was Queen Elizabeth of York, and certainly she should know about being a pawn. I hate to think she was right, but my life has never been in my control, even though I'm the son of John Dudley, 1st Duke of Northumberland, and Jane Guilford, and the husband of the only nine-day Queen of England!

Let me explain. When my father wanted something, he went for it by any means available. Some would say that he was guilty of the crime of ambition. My mother tried to explain it to me once, "It's in his blood. After Henry VIII had his father executed, John and his family were desperate. But then we married, he was knighted during a French campaign, and he rose steadily from then on. He got it all back. He became Lord High Admiral, Master of the Horse, Viscount Lisle…."

"And the Earl of Warwick," I interrupted.

"And the Duke of Northumberland," retorted my mother.

"Yes and then he managed to oust Somerset, the Lord Protector of England and Governor of the King's Person, and govern England in the name of Edward VI without Parliament or Council," added my older brother John, entering the room.

In walked my father. "You see, Guilford, when Henry VIII died, he left three children by three different mothers. His heir, nine-year-old Edward VI is a major supporter of the Protestant faith as is Elizabeth, his half-sister. Princess Mary, who some would consider the legitimate heir, is Roman Catholic." His eyebrow wiggled with disdain.

"But I hear you and others talking. Why do we have to worry about this?"

"I expect that my sons will always work for the good of the Dudley family." He looked significantly at me, but he didn't say anything."

Mother said, "Isn't Edward quite ill?"

Father replied, "It doesn't look like Edward will make old bones. If he dies and Princess Mary takes over, she will demand that England return to the Catholic faith. She will also demand the return of the former church properties that Henry VIII gave to others and me when he closed the Roman Catholic monasteries."

"That is our inheritance, Guilford," John added. "Of course, as the fifth and youngest son, you might not get any!"

"Mother will take care of me, won't you?" I winked at Mother. She smiled back. I knew I was her favorite.

Turning to our father, my brother John continued, "But you're the leader of the Privy Council and have easy access to Edward so you can figure out how to change the line of succession, can't you?"

"Very good, John. That's exactly what I'm doing with a few good friends. Edward has signed a new order of succession, which rules out both Mary and Elizabeth, and designates Henry VIII's grandniece Lady Jane Grey, the fourth in line for the Crown of England, as his successor."

"That's very nice, dear. Both Edward and she were brought up by Katherine Parr, Henry VIII's last Queen." Mother smiled happily.

"Isn't she that really smart but very short girl?" John asked.

"Yes, she knows Latin, Greek and Hebrew, generally wears black and white, and appears to be most religious," my mother said.

My father always had his eye on his goal. Later, he told me that he had arranged that I would marry Jane, a member of the royal house. I thought that would be rather grand having a royal bride, although Lady Jane Grey did not appear to be interested in men. She was only sixteen, but she really seemed to like her religious leanings more than the opposite sex. But that didn't matter to our parents. By placing the two of us on the throne after Edward died, our parents thought they would be in control. My father, the chess master, was all-powerful, and Jane would be his puppet Queen.

In May of 1553, Jane and I married, even though she didn't want me and considered me the son of a self-seeking opportunistic tyrant, which I thought very unfair of her. We had a grand wedding, although I embarrassed myself by throwing up the best Rhenish.

My father planned well. Edward died in July—only six weeks later—and he had Jane proclaimed Queen of England. She first collapsed on the floor, crying. Then she told him that the Lady Mary was the rightful heir, and my father told her she wronged herself and her family. Her parents ordered her to do what she was told. I tried to persuade her, but all she would agree to do was pray for guidance. So while everyone watched, she begged God to give her a sign. Finally, she yielded and sat on the throne. Everyone sighed with relief. She may have resisted, but they had won again.

The next day the trumpeters blew a fanfare, and royal heralds declared her Queen in Westminister, Cheapside, and other places in London, but no one cheered. When we arrived at the Tower, the guns saluted Jane. But no one seemed particularly pleased, which was a shame. We were dressed for the occasion; I was wearing white, gold, and silver, and Jane was wearing green and white, the Tudor colors, and high-heeled shoes to give her more height. We proceeded though the Tower to the main entrance to the royal towers. Once we were welcomed, those who were present and we attended a service in the Chapel of St. John. That evening there was a huge banquet and mulled wine. Then someone arrived with a letter from Princess Mary, who had escaped capture. Although my father and others laughed and said that Mary wouldn't be a problem, the banquet was ruined.

Later that night, Jane announced, "I will not make you King, you know."

"What! Of course, I will be King."

"Never," and she turned away. I was incensed. I wanted to go back home with Mother, but then Jane said I had to stay by her side.

Meanwhile, Mary Tudor proclaimed her right to the throne. The first Queen to rule England, she was met by wildly cheering crowds in villages and towns as she progressed across the country to London. When she entered London through Aldgate on August 3, bells rang and people cheered their support for Henry VIII's first-born and danced in the streets. She then imprisoned Jane and me, our parents and our supporters. Mary Tudor was the next Queen of England. As Queen, just like my father feared, she intended to restore England to the Roman Catholic Church.

The Queen had my father executed. As sons of an executed traitor, my brothers, John, Ambrose, Robert, Henry, and I were assigned to cheerless stone chambers in the Tower. We passed our time carving inscriptions and pictures on the walls. I even carved Jane's name, even though she didn't like me very much. She liked her books much better.

Although Jane and I were found guilty of high treason, Mary refused to execute us. That was most fortunate for I was sentenced to be hanged, drawn, and quartered at the Queen's pleasure. Jane was to be burned alive or beheaded. Mary agreed to spare our lives, and for six months we lived

The Tower of London, a UNESCO World Heritage Site, is immersed in history. It has ghosts, kings and queens and their families, jewels, ravens and many stories. *Courtesy of D. Peter Lund*

in the Tower. We were housed separately; I was shut up in the freezing Beauchamp Tower.

In 1554, when Mary insisted on marrying Philip of Spain, the Kentish rebel Thomas Wyatt advanced on London. Once he was arrested, Queen Mary and the Council decided that Wyatt and other leaders of the rebellion would have to die–and for the safety and stability of her kingdom, Jane and I would have to be executed. Princess Elizabeth, the next heir to the throne, was imprisoned in the Tower of London. Being in line for the throne means that you have to be very careful.

It really isn't fair. I never got to be King. Jane and I were the innocent victims of our parents' ambition. In less than two days, my living body will cease to exist. Jane will be beheaded on Tower Green, while I, since I am not of royal blood, will be beheaded on Tower Hill. I pray that the executioner has a steady hand and that I have the strength to lie my head down on the block without showing fear.

I wanted to say farewell to Jane, but she told me instead "We will shortly behold each other in a better place." Hah.

I wept on my way to Tower Hill, but when I got there, I shook hands with my friends and knelt in prayer. I asked everyone to pray for me as they bandaged my eyes.

Only one swing of the ax was necessary to remove my head. The guards carried my body to the historic Chapel Royal of St. Peter ad Vincula in the grounds of the Tower. On seeing the body from her window, Jane is alleged to have cried, "Oh, Guilford, Guilford." Jane and I are buried under the chapel flagstones. My brothers were subsequently pardoned.

Since that time, Guilford's ghost has been seen weeping silently in the Beauchamp Tower, where he awaited his execution. On February 12, 1957, on the 403rd anniversary of her execution, two Guardsmen saw Lady Jane Grey's ghost. There are also reports of light poltergeist activity and soft gasps.

**Directions:** Take the Underground to Tower Hill and follow the signs.

# My Father

*The past is never dead. It's not even past.*

William Faulkner

## House of Stuart and Oliver Cromwell

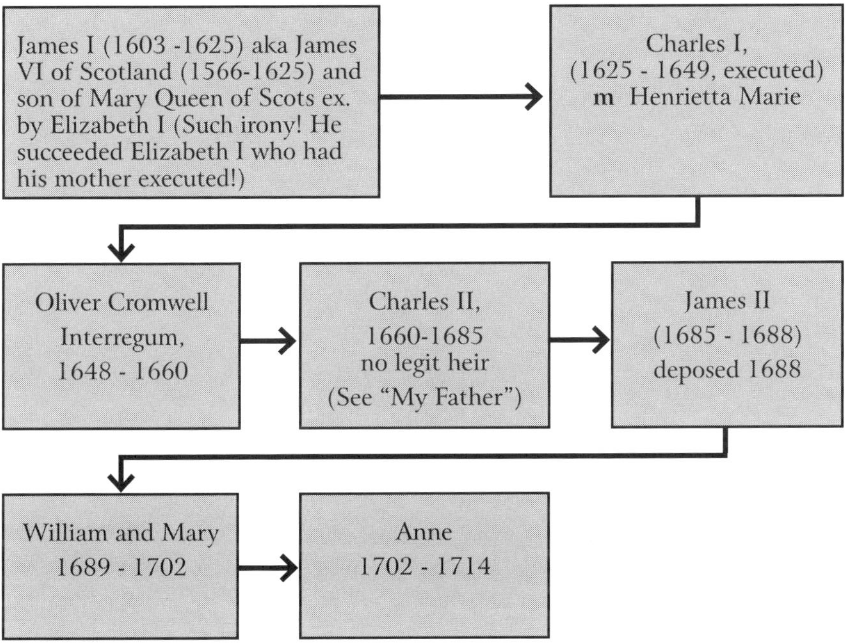


There are some people who insist that every time one door closes, another door opens; but that is not always true. There are doors that are meant to stay closed, the ones that lead to rooms filled with sorrow and pain. If we have lived awhile, most of us have at least one room like that.

I do, even on a beautiful day like today. I should point out, though, that May 29, 1660, is a day of great significance for me. It's the day when I return to my people, the day I enter my capital, London, and my thirtieth birthday. A fitting day for my return from twelve years of exile.

Today, the bells ring from every tower and steeple. Cannons boom and fountains run with wine. The crowds are massive. People line the roads. They are hugging and embracing. "Those days of grey drab are long gone," one shouts. "Our Charlie is back," cries another. "The Roundheads are gone," calls a third. Drums and trumpets play fervently.

Life was not much fun under the humorless Cromwell. A highly religious man, he believed that if you worked hard you would get to heaven. He closed the theaters, banned sports, enforced law through the military–the list goes on. Now, I enter London with gilded royal coaches, 20,000 soldiers, silver-clothed gentlemen, and purple and green-dressed servants, trumpeters, and heralds. The Lord Mayor, aldermen, and members of city companies in their various liveries and gold chains are marching about. Colored banners flap in the breeze while trumpets, fifes and drums play. My Cavaliers march along beside me. It is a day of festivity and of great celebration.

I ride bareheaded, smiling at this one and that and winking at the pretty faces. I do love all those pretty women. I have long dreamed of this day, but I always thought that blood would have to be shed to bring it about. Certainly, I never thought that the very army that sent my father to the block and kept me in exile would ask for my return.

But now I am back, and the long black dresses and white headdresses have been ripped off. Dresses reveal feminine charms, and men's clothes vie with women's in their ostentation. Women wear make-up and bright colors. There are so many people and so many signs of loyal homage that it is seven o'clock before I arrive at Whitehall. By this time, the bonfires have been lit and windows display lighted candles. It's my own fault that I have been away so long, as I met no one "who did not protest that he had ever wished for my return."

As I enter the palace, the irony strikes me. Here, my father had commissioned Sir Peter Paul Rubens to paint a ceiling commemorating the reign of his father, James I, in 1634; and here in 1649, my father walked under that ceiling, out a modified window, to his execution.

In the years I have been gone, life has changed tremendously. For the first eight years of my life, I was heir apparent and all was well. By 1642, my father's reign was a political and financial disaster and civil war was brewing. He talked about the divine right of Kings, and the people feared that he was trying to gain absolute power. He levied taxes without Parliament's consent, and the people were outraged.

Originally a part of Whitehall Palace, the Banqueting House contains Peter Paul Ruben's only surviving in-situ ceiling painting commissioned by Charles I. The ceiling was one of Charles I's last sights before he lost his head. Indigo Jones designed the Banqueting House in the new Palladian style of architecture in 1622. *Courtesy of D. Peter Lund*

Money shortages and the stubbornness of men brought my father to this place. His subjects did not believe as he did in the divine right of Kings. He argued that God had given him the right and that Kings cannot do wrong, for they are divine. Essentially, the Parliamentarians did not agree.

I was only twelve when we marched north to York to raise an Army; Civil War broke out between my father and Parliament in 1642; my mother, Henrietta Maria, and siblings were in safety in France. I first saw action at the Battle of Edgehill, where the Roundheads almost captured me. Generally, though, I was based at Oxford in the Cavalier headquarters. Father allowed me to accompany him on his campaigns in 1643 and 1644, but he had said I could not participate in the battle. After Father was defeated at Naseby, he made me seek refuge in France, with my mother, sisters, and brothers.

By 1649, Father had lost two civil wars and was the prisoner of his rebellious subjects. After three days of meeting and prayer, Cromwell and his army had decided to call my father to account for the "mischief he had done to his utmost against the Lord's causes and the people." (Coote, p. 64). While I was trying to save my father's life through diplomatic means, his trial was taking place in Westminister Hall. He sat in a crimson velvet chair in the body of the hall facing the sixty-seven commissioners, who, under Cromwell, had taken over the running of the country. Cromwell –not my father – sat in the royal chair of state, beneath the arms of the Commonwealth, which had replaced the royal arms. The charge accused my father of being responsible for the evil brought upon England and the death of innocent people.

I was in Holland then–sent there for my safety. While I watched helplessly from the Continent, Father was found guilty of treason. The Court decreed that he was a tyrant, traitor,

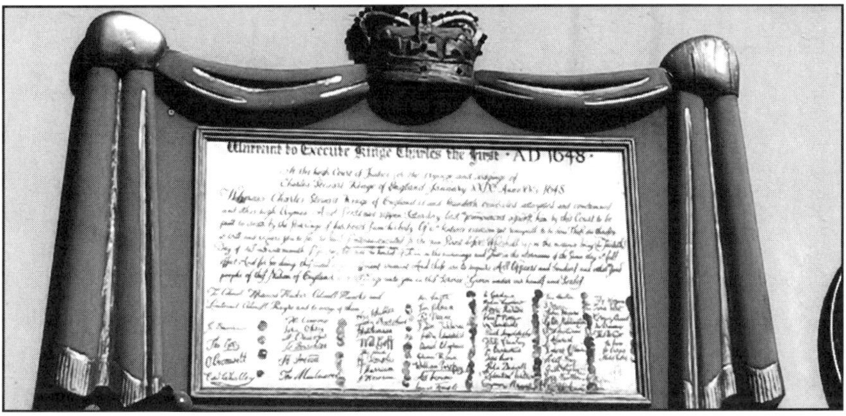


A copy of the warrant for the execution of Charles I is displayed outside the former Old Kings Head in Windsor. Cromwell's signature (#3 above) is one of the easiest to make out on the death warrant of Charles I. Supposedly, the guards protecting Charles' dead body saw a shadowy man, who was heard to mutter, "T'was a cruel necessity, t'was a cruel necessity." Perhaps this was Cromwell? *Courtesy of D. Peter Lund*

murderer, and public enemy to the people of England and should be put to death by the severing of his head from his body.

On January 30, 1649, great crowds began to stand in front of the Banqueting Hall. Before ten o'clock in the morning, the distant roll of drums could be heard and those on rooftops could see two long files of soldiers stretching all the way back to St. James Palace; between them stood the small figure of my father, Charles I. Drums beat and colors flew. At Whitehall, they conducted him to a private room. At two o'clock, his captors led him through the palace galleries to the Banqueting Hall, where he had requested that Rubens paint that glorious ceiling. From there, he stepped directly on the black-draped scaffold, from an upstairs window specially removed for this event. In the center of it stood the block and the axe. Companies of soldiers surrounded the scaffold, vast crowds filled Whitehall, and spectators occupied every available window, balcony and roof. My father lay down at full length and prayed as the watchers silently waited. When he spread his arms wide, the executioner brought down the great ax, and the body of the lifeless King of England sprawled at the feet of the executioner. The assistant executioner raised the severed head high so all could see, proclaiming loudly, "Behold the head of a traitor. So die all traitors." They say the assembled multitude groaned – was it in horror of what had been done – the execution of a King?

Nearly a week after the execution, I learned of my father's death when another exile addressed me as "Your Majesty." That was when I grew up. I was a King without a country, a son without a father, a man left adrift. In London, my father's body was placed in a coffin; after embalming, it was displayed so the public could pay their last respects. Of course, I wasn't there. Early in February, his coffin was taken to St. George's Chapel at Windsor Castle and lowered into the vault, which holds the bodies of Henry VIII and his third wife, Jane Seymour.

The Scots offered to put me on the Scottish throne if I became a Presbyterian. I finally accepted and set sail for Scotland, where I was crowned King of Scotland in January 1651. Within a year, we encountered Cromwell's army at the Battle of Worcester. The Scots fought with amazing courage, knowing that the Parliamentarians would show little mercy. After one of their commanders had his head blown off, I assumed command of his forces. Two horses were killed under me; then Cromwell's soldiers pursued our army into the city. We were losing, and I was finally persuaded to escape. Up to 3,000 Scots were killed during the battle and around 10,000 taken prisoner, many of whom were transported as forced laborers to New England. Supposedly, the Parliamentarian army lost only 200 men.

For the next six weeks, the Roundheads hounded me – a twenty-one-year-old King – on the run through the south of

England. Since the Parliamentary-wanted posters described me as a tall dark man – which I was – I had to disguise myself. I cut my long hair short, exchanged clothes with a peasant, and spoke with a country accent. I threw away my uncomfortable boots – that weren't made for walking – and walked in my stockinged feet. Perhaps one of the most exciting moments was when I hid in an oak tree with a supply of bread, beer and cheese and remained there warm and safe while the Roundheads searched below. I donned a sober grey suit and stove pipe hat and rode pillion – right through a troop of Roundheads. Finally, I got back to safety.

I probably wouldn't be alive today if I remained at Worcester. Cromwell would have killed me or stuck me in the Tower to waste away. Luckily, I was spared so one day I could reopen the door, marked King of England.

I spent the next nine years of my life as a penniless nomad, roaming Europe, looking for people who would help me regain my throne. I also became a great fan of women, whom I so happily bed. I had at least five mistresses and one son and daughter before I was recalled to England. Almost any woman I desired was mine for the asking.

On September 3, 1658, Cromwell died. The ostentatious mourning was a lot more than my poor father received. Hooded mourners, black-draped horses, and the slow beating of military drums accompanied the hearse. Cromwell was buried in Henry VII's Chapel at Westminster Abbey, the usual burial place of Kings and Queens of England until that date. He had bequeathed the Protectorate to his son, Richard Cromwell, who had no aptitude for government. Accordingly, General Monck proposed that the monarchy – my monarchy – be restored. I promised to call a free parliament to settle all the problems facing the country. I assured people of every religion that they would be given liberty of conscience. I made other promises, and the Convention Parliament invited me to return and resume my inheritance. So nineteen months later I have returned. Now it is my turn to be a King for my people.

I still mourn my father, but punishing his killers doesn't make his death better. Although I didn't want to reopen old wounds by castigating the men who had voted for the execution of my father, Parliament insisted on having them tried. Only twenty-eight survivors appeared in the dock of the Old Bailey. Ten were sentenced to death, but in their eyes they had committed no murder; they had carried out the demands of justice. I went to the execution of Major General Thomas Harrison, one of the regicides who had sentenced my father to death. At Charing Cross, Harrison swung from the gallows for several minutes. Half choking, he was then stretched on the boards for the executioner to slit open his stomach and pull out his entrails. Within seconds, his head was removed and his intestines thrown on the fire. Retribution had been done. My ministers wanted them all dead as did the people. So I let them die, but enough have died and I'm weary of hanging.

I urged instead that the Convention punish those who were already dead – my father's true enemies. On January 30, 1661, the anniversary of my father's execution, the government unceremoniously disinterred the bodies of Cromwell and two other leaders. They were drawn in a hurdle to Tyburn, where after hanging for some hours, they were beheaded. Their bodies were buried under the gallows, and their heads stuck on spikes outside Westminister Hall, where they were exhibited for many years. Cromwell's head remained for over forty years.

Yes, many doors have closed in my life. I'm no longer that poverty-stricken King without a throne. Life will be quite splendid now, but the horrific death of my father is a room that still haunts me. A King was executed; does that mean other Kings can face a similar fate at the hands of their subjects?

Situated on the north bank of the River Thames, the Royal Palace of Westminister is the Parliament of the United Kingdom. Once the home of the royal family and still officially a royal palace, most of the buildings that now make up the modern Houses of Parliament were rebuilt after a fire in 1834. *Courtesy of Thomas P. Rooney*

*On April 23, 1661, Charles II was crowned King at Westminster Abbey. Following his father's execution, Cromwell had ordered that the royal regalia 'be totally broken' as being symbolic of the 'detestable rule of Kings'. The regalia's precious stones were sold separately and the precious metal sent to the mint to be coined, although other pieces (such as the Coronation Spoon dating from the twelfth century and later returned to Charles II) were sold intact. The Coronation Chair (dating from 1300) also remained intact as it was used in 1653 at Westminster Hall when Cromwell was installed as Lord Protector. A new set of royal regalia was made for the occasion*

*The ghost of Charles I's regicide remains with us forever. During the Stuart period in England, Kings were presumed to have the divine authority to rule. In bringing Charles I to trial and executing him, the people were challenging his divine right to rule and, therefore, God's will. A precedent was set that day. A little more than hundred years later, King Louis XVI and his Queen Maria Antoinette were guillotined in Paris. Other Kings have suffered similar fates subsequently.*

**Directions:** The closest tube station is Westminster, via District, Circle or Jubilee lines.

# The Headless Valet

With so many famous people having lived under its roof, St. James's Palace has its share of ghosts. Completed in 1536, St. James's Palace has been a royal residence for over three hundred years. Much of the original red brick building, including the Chapel Royal, the gatehouse, some turrets and two Tudor rooms in the State apartments, survive to this day. The great Tudor Gatehouse at the southern end of St. James's Street still bears Henry VIII's royal cipher HR, surmounted by his crown.

Henry Fitzroy, the only illegitimate offspring that Henry VIII recognized, lived in the palace. Henry even considered making him a legitimate heir and made him Lord President of the Council of the North and Warden of the West, Middle and East Scottish Marches. Unfortunately, Fitzroy died in the palace at the age of seventeen from tuberculosis.

Subsequently, other members of royalty lived there. Anne Boleyn stayed there the night after her coronation, and Elizabeth I resided there during the Spanish Armada attack. Mary I surrendered Calais while residing there. Stuart Kings were born and baptized there. Many of the Hanovers lived there after Whitehall Palace burned in 1698. William IV was the last sovereign to use St. James's Palace as a residence.

But now back to the ghosts of St. James. One of the most horrifying is the ghost of a valet who trails blood from the gaping wound in his throat. He walks the halls late at night. This ghost dates back to May 31, 1810, when Ernest Augustus, Duke of Cumberland, fifth son of George III (remember the War for American Independence?), and brother to George IV and William IV, was in residence. An ardent Tory and a fanatic anti-Catholic, Cumberland opposed the Catholic

Emancipation Bill and was a founding member of the anti-Catholic Orange Order. He and his sister Sophie were rumored to have had an incestuous relationship. It is unclear whether there was truth to these rumors, or whether they were circulated by Whigs to damage the Duke. He is also alleged to have assaulted the wife of Lord Lyndhurst.

Most English castles have at least one ghost. A bloody, almost headless ghost haunts St. James' Palace. *Courtesy of D. Peter Lund*

The story goes like this. Cumberland says a noise in his bedroom awoke him around 2:30 am. Wearing his white nightcap and gown, he began to rise from his bed when a sharp-bladed weapon slashed at him. He tried to defend himself, suffering cuts on his hands and wrists. When he screamed, Cornelius Neale, a valet, rushed in. He found the Duke's blood-soaked regimental saber lying on the floor by the door. No one else was in the room – according to the story.

As a doctor treated his wounds, Cumberland asked that someone send for his other valet, Joseph Sellis. Two servants went to rouse Sellis, but as they approached his room, they heard a peculiar gurgling sound. Rushing in, they found Sellis with his throat cut so severely that they could see his spinal cord. His head was almost severed from his body. At the inquest, a theory was offered that Sellis had, for reasons unknown, attempted to kill Cumberland. Feeling guilty, he then retreated to his room where he killed himself.

Knowing Cumberland's reputation, courtiers thought differently. Several hinted that the facts had been misconstrued. More than one thought that Cumberland had murdered Sellis. Sellis' hands were clean, they pointed out, and his washbasin contained bloodstained water. Would Sellis have had the time or the opportunity to wash his hands, having almost cut his head off? And how does one cut off one's own head? Doesn't seem feasible, does it? That's what the courtiers thought.

They soon developed several alternative scenarios as to what really happened. One version maintained that Sellis had found the Duke in bed with his wife. The Duke had killed him to prevent him from exposing his adultery. Another version said that Cumberland had seduced Sellis' daughter, who became pregnant. She then committed suicide. When Sellis confronted his employer, Cumberland killed the valet to avert the possibility of a scandal. Mid-nineteenth century "armchair detectives" hypothesized that the Duke and the other valet, Neale, were involved in 'the grossest and most unnatural immorality,' and that Cumberland ordered the murder of Sellis, who caught them *in flagrante delicto*.

Alas, to this day, Sellis is the legal culprit and so he walks the halls. Despite this bloody, almost headless specter, St. James Palace is the home of several members of the Royal Family and their household offices. It is often in use for official functions and is not open to the public.

**Directions:** Exit St. James's Park Station, cross Old Queen Street, turn left on Birdcage Walk and cross St. James Park. Cross the Mall on to St. James Street.

# Buckingham Ghosts

*Most English castles harbor one or two ghosts within their solid stonewalls. Maybe the actual building with its solid walls and that marvelous turreted roofline serves to preserve those ghostly echoes through time. Certainly, castles have seen a great deal of history and in many cases one or two bodies are or were secluded in various nooks and crannies.*

In the early seventeen hundreds, the location of Buckingham Palace was an uninviting site surrounded by marshes fed by the Tyburn River. There, John Sheffield, Duke of Buckingham, built a large townhouse in 1703.

One ghost goes back in time to when the site contained a priory. Every Christmas Day, a monk appears on a terrace of Buckingham Palace overlooking the gardens. Supposedly, he died in the monastery's punishment cell. Bound in heavy chains and dressed in brown, he moans on the terrace, dragging his chains backwards and forwards for a few minutes before fading into nothingness – not to be seen again until the next Christmas.

In 1761, the newly crowned George III bought Buckingham House as a private residence for his wife Queen Charlotte. It soon became known as the Queen's House – although the children's house might have been more appropriate – fourteen of George III's fifteen children were born there.

On his accession in 1820, George IV decided he needed a pied-à-terre. As work progressed, the King decided to transform the house into a palace. The north and south wings of Buckingham House were rebuilt on a larger scale to celebrate the British victories at Trafalgar and Waterloo. The Marble Arch became the triumphal showpiece of the enlarged courtyard.

Queen Victoria was the first sovereign to live in the palace. To provide a children's nursery and guest bedrooms, a fourth wing was built – once the Marble Arch was moved.

At Buckingham Palace, a chained monk appears every Christmas Day. Gunshots are heard in another part of the palace. *Courtesy of D. Peter Lund*

The present forecourt of the Palace, where the Changing the Guard takes place, was completed just before the First World War. The Royal Collection Department reported in 1999 that the palace contained 19 staterooms, 52 principal bedrooms, 188 staff bedrooms, 92 offices and 78 bathrooms.

The palace has a second and more contemporary ghost, dating from the reign of Edward VII (1901-1910). Major John Gwynne, the King's private secretary, was involved in a scandalous divorce that meant he was shunned by polite society. Feeling deeply ashamed, he retired one night to his first-floor office, pulled out his revolver and blew out his brains. Since that day, staff members working in the vicinity have occasionally heard a gun firing from that room.

The palace's staterooms are open to visitors during August and September. They contain many of the greatest treasures from the Royal Collection — paintings by Rembrandt, Rubens, Vermeer, Poussin, and Canaletto; sculptures by Canova and

Chantrey; exquisite examples of Sèvres porcelain; and some of the finest English and French furniture in the world.

**Directions:** Buckingham Palace is accessible by Victoria, Green Park, and Hyde Park Corner underground stations.

# Death's Messenger

*Sometimes the dead aren't really the dead.*

Once upon a time in nineteenth century London, there were two sisters who lived together in a yellow house at 19 St. James Place. Ann and Harriet loved each other devotedly and did everything together. They even looked alike with their sharp noses, wasp waists, which were really due to their tightly laced corsets, and their vast number of starched and flounced petticoats. Their bodices had high necks and long sleeves and were buttoned up the front; their feet were shod in tightly laced boots.

They had always lived together – ever since they were little girls. Although Ann was one year older than Harriet, they shared the same bedroom with its mahogany furniture. Their matching well figured serpentine chests had shaped sides and molded edges above two short and three long drawers. Their four-posted beds required stools to climb into. When their mother died, they wore black attire for one year and rarely saw their father. Their grandmother gave them each a bracelet of plaited hair removed from the head of their dead mother.

Their governess, Miss Adams, commanded respect, not only from Ann and Harriet but also from the household servants and their father. When their father was away, which was often for many months, she was left in complete control of her charges. Severe and strict, she was not only concerned with the education of the two girls but also all aspects of their upbringing, including their moral standards and values. Unfortunately, her discipline sometimes required a leather strap. Lessons with Miss Adams included morning prayers, scriptures, writing and dictation, arithmetic, geography and composition with fifteen minutes for recreation in the morning and afternoon. She emphasized recitation and required the girls to memorize a psalm each week. The girls were punished for spelling mistakes, sloppy handwriting or not doing their work.

Her rules focused on their manners. She would tell them to always behave respectfully, be kind to others and never be rude, keep the Sabbath holy, remain neat and tidy in appearance and care for all their belongings.

Sometimes she took the girls to visit the zoo, museums, exhibitions and art galleries. She emphasized walking for their constitution. "Walking," said she, "is man's best medicine according to Hippocrates." At home they played with a range of toys from wax dolls to doll houses.

When they were sixteen, their father said they were too old for a governess, and Miss Adams left. Their world now consisted of their father, when he was around, and each other. Their grandmother was dead, and they knew few people. Neither married. When their father died, they felt a sense of freedom.

Every morning they got up at the same time. At 11 am, they donned their bonnets and shawls and took an hour's constitutional on the crowded city streets. They walked past the Georgian and Regency terraces with their network of mews or alleys where carriages were stored and horses stabled. They picked up their skirts when they came to the steaming piles of horse manure in the streets and sniffed daintily. They primly walked past the street vendors hawking their wares, the pickpockets, prostitutes, drunks, beggars and street sweepers. If they met up with an organ grinder, they marveled at the reversing cylinders and all those needles! Then they returned to their yellow house to ensure that their servant had washed their dishes and made their beds with square corners.

Together, the two sisters dared to take small adventures. They talked about the scramble for Africa, the hazardous journeys and settlements of the Christian missionaries as

London streets in the nineteenth century. *Courtesy of D. Peter Lund*

they spread the Gospel to faraway places such as Malta, Aden, Colombo, and Hong Kong. When the Great Exhibition opened in the Crystal Palace in Hyde Park, they went to see the cast iron and glass building. They delighted in the beautiful, ethereal building and its contents. More than 14,000 exhibitors from around the world had come to exhibit examples of the latest technology developed in the Industrial Revolution. Afterwards, they found that they were more fascinated by the scientific instruments, the machines such as McCormick's Reaper, than the decorative arts. Soon they forgot about it because gold was found in Australia.

Devoted to each other, they finished each other's sentences, read each other's journals and discussed the authors of the day: Thackeray, Dickens, and even that American Melville. They enjoyed their meals of fowl and joint of mutton, plum pudding and *blanc mange*. Sometimes their nieces Mrs. Mary Coppinger and Miss Emma Pearson and their nephew's wife,

Mrs. Alice Pearson, visited. Life was good because they had each other.

But then, the day came when that was no longer true. Ann died in 1858, and Harriet lived alone in the house. As is wont to happen when people are older and living alone, the house became quite shabby. Books were piled up in corners. Glasses were left on tables. A smell of unwashed linen permeated the house. When Harriet's nieces visited, they often found her talking to Ann.

"Ann says we should read that new *Moby Dick* by Melville," Harriet would announce. "She thinks we will enjoy it thoroughly."

"Ann tells me that it is your birthday, Emma," and she would hand over a badly wrapped box containing a pair of old gloves.

The nieces were somewhat disconcerted when she poured a cup of tea for Ann, but they agreed that other than this mild dottiness, she seemed all right. "Of course," sniffed Alice, "she hasn't changed her bodice for weeks. Look at the food stains on it."

"What I find more unpleasant is that wretched smell," commented Mary. "Rather like something died in the scullery."

"I think something did – like a very fat mouse! I found its carcass."

Harriet lived alone in the house for six years. In November 1864, she fell ill in Brighton while on vacation with Mrs. Coppinger, Miss Emma Pearson, and Mrs. John Pearson. They brought her back to London and nursed her carefully. After all, there were no other heirs.

On December 23, heavy snow began to fall in the street outside, and a thick mist swirled around the windows of the house. Mary and Emma went to bed, leaving their door open and the gaslight burning on the stair landing. Alice Pearson

No 19, St. James Place, is the site of one haunting.
*Courtesy of D. Peter Lund*

remained awake to watch over the sick Harriet. At about one in the morning, both heard footsteps coming up the stairs. Then they saw their dead Aunt Ann go past their open door and into Harriet's room. Rushing out of that room, Mrs. Pearson said, "Come quickly. I just saw Ann."

All three women returned to their aunt's bedside. Harriet smiled at them, "I've just seen Ann. She has come to collect me and take me away." Harriet shut her eyes and breathed a long, blissful sigh. She died at 6 am with a beatific smile on her face.

**Directions:** From the Green Park Station, walk along Queens Walk and make a right on Piccadilly. Make a right on St. James Street, turn right on St. James Place and turn right at the very end.

# LEGENDS

Legends are stories that have been passed down for generations. Often, they are presented as history, but they are not necessarily true. They are believable but not necessarily believed. When it comes to legends about the world of ghosts, it is even harder to know what is true or what to believe: are there curses, people rising from the dead, or evil spirits? Who knows?

# The Miserly Ferryman

*And so over the fields to Southwarke. I spent half an hour in St Mary Overy's church, where are fine monuments of great antiquity.*
Samuel Pepys - 21st July 1663

At one point, the River Thames, which was not confined to its present bed, spread into many marshes. A ferry was the only way to cross the river with its many tributaries because the people of that time did not know how to make a bridge that long.

John Overs, a ferryman, lived in a timber frame house set on stone foundations on the south bank of the Thames River close to the present London Bridge. He charged two pence to transport an ordinary passenger across the river and twelve for a knight with his horse. John had become exceedingly rich through his ferry, but he was a notorious skinflint.

His only daughter, the gentle, fair-headed Mary, had a suitor for her hand, but John refused to provide her with a dowry. "If I give you a dowry, I lose my money and my help around my home," said John. In those days, a woman's prospect for a suitable husband was greatly handicapped unless she had an appropriate dowry. Without a dowry, Mary was stuck with her tight-fisted, mean-tempered father.

So were John's servants. In those days, being a servant was a respectable occupation. A boy from a poor family could improve his standing financially and socially if he found employment as a servant in a rich man's house. A servant could save his money and move on—but not in John's house. He was rich, but he did not pay his servants well and fed them poorly.

His servants ate and drank whatever he gave them because that was all they had. He fed them stale bread with weevils, day-old lamprey and scrawny chickens. His ale was thin, and rarely did he allow them any meat. Meanwhile, he complained that they were "eating him out of house and home."

One day, John decided he needed to augment his considerable savings. "If I feign death for twenty-four hours," he thought, "my daughter and servants will have to mourn me." In those days, mourning meant that everyone fasted as part of their grieving. He thought to himself, "When they fast, I will save the cost of food for one day. That's a lot of money." Pleased by this realization, he wrapped himself in his burial shroud and climbed into a coffin in the main room of his house.

But John's servants didn't grieve, nor did his daughter Mary, who visited a friend. Once she was gone, the servants promptly unlocked the pantry and celebrated his death with a great feast. Out came the good ale, the ham, the bread and cheese, the smoked fish, and dried fruit. They ate and drank, told jokes, sang songs, and ate and drank again. John lay still in the coffin for as long as he could, but eventually their celebration roused his wrath. He sat up, seizing the first weapon at hand, and attacked one of his servants. Horrified by the rising of his dead master, another servant shouted, "The devil is rising in my master's body," and struck out John's brains with an oar.

On learning that her father had died for yet a second time, Mary sent word to her suitor that finally she had a dowry and they could be married. Her lover, in his rush to reach her, was killed when his horse stumbled and threw him. Although the beautiful Mary had many offers of marriage after that, she decided that God was telling

Southwark Cathedral is situated on the south bank of the River Thames close to London Bridge. Some believe that there has been a church here for over a thousand years. *Courtesy of D. Peter Lund*

her that she should not be married. Instead, she established a House of Sisters, calling it Mary Audrey, with the saintly prefix. Over time, Audrey became corrupted into "Overie" and the house became known as St. Mary Overies!

Subsequently, the House of Sisters was converted into a priory. Not wanting to be in the ferry business, the priests built a timber bridge, which became London Bridge. Since 1905, the priory has been Southwark Cathedral.

**Directions:** Cross over London Bridge. Go right down the second set of steps into the grounds of Southwark Cathedral.

# The Noble Wife

*The woman is subject to man on account of the weakness of her nature . . . Man is the beginning of woman and her end, just as God is the beginning and end of every creature. Children ought to love their father more than they love their mother.*

St. Thomas of Aquinas, 1225-1274

In the medieval days in England, as in the twenty-first century, greed was a problem. In that time, everyone wanted land. If they couldn't have land, they wanted silver or gold. To get what they wanted, nobles would seize each other's castles and abuse their servants and family members. Sometimes, they would hire mercenaries and ruffians to attack their enemies. They would plunder, ransack, and pillage. They would torture others to extract large ransoms. Meanwhile, the King, who often was not much better, would heap rewards and privileges on the treacherous nobles, if they pleased him.

The eldest son in his family, Roger de Mandeville had been trained as a warrior and a knight. When he had completed his training, he was knighted and swore his allegiance to the King. He then married the beautiful Hilda, who owned land in Enfield Chace and moved there to avoid the strife and intrigue at court.

Roger and Hilda were the local lord and lady of the Enfield Chace region. Roger enjoyed the small but nicely turreted castle that was his wife's dowry. He heard reports regarding the estate crops, harvests and supplies. After early morning mass, he rode into the village and collected the rents that were owed him and ensured that the King's taxes were paid on time. He oversaw the building and maintenance of roads, bridges and fortifications. He exercised his judicial powers over his vassals and peasants, heard complaints, and settled disputes. As a leader in war, he was responsible for the raising, equipping and training of the local army, drawn from among all his dependents, who were bound to him by fealty and homage.

Roger knew that a good marriage could bring considerable economic benefits. His marriage contract required detailed planning by his parents, but in the end he not only acquired land and chattels but also the beautiful Hilda, whom he loved. The law gave him full rights over his wife who effectively became his property.

The church had taught Hilda that women were inferior to men and that she should be meek and obedient to her husband. She looked after children and saw to such tasks as cooking and making clothes. She also hired the laborers, supervised the stewards, sold the wheat, oats and rye, and kept the accounts.

In three years, Roger and Hilda had three sons: William, Henry, and John. After that, Hilda took care not to get pregnant, saying to herself that three large strapping sons in three years were enough for any man and woman. They cared for their family and friends, worked hard on their estate, and loved each other well. When evening came, they looked at each other in the dim light cast by rush lights over the long refectory table in the hall, tossed their scraps to the dogs, and smiled with contentment. At night, they slept in each other's arms, both gently snoring.

Medieval Britain placed great importance on an individual's status in society. Roger knew that if his sons were to succeed that they too had to train for knighthood. Of course, William, the oldest, was the most important because he would inherit the estate, while his brothers would enter the church or become landless knights hoping to marry into wealth. When William reached the age of seven, Roger told Hilda that he was sending him away to live in the castle of his liege lord.

Hilda burst into tears. "He's too young. He's not ready to go."

"You're not ready to let him go, my dear wife. You will spoil him further if he stays home with us. He will become proud and arrogant. I heard him boasting to his brothers the other day that he was a wonderful knight."

"But he will be."

"He will be—when he has served as a page, taking care of his master's armor, equipment, and horses. I know that you have taught him the rudiments of singing and dancing. He knows how to ride a horse, and we have practiced the use of his sword. But now he needs to leave us."

So William went off to learn virtue and chivalry. He received religious instruction from the chaplain and training in arms from the squires. His mistress and her ladies taught him to honor and protect all women. He also learned to play the lute, to hunt and to hawk. At the age of fourteen, he became a squire and learned to handle the sword and lance and to bear the weight of heavy armor. In addition to his other duties, he now had to carve at the dinner table and to accompany his knight to war. William's job was to assist him in putting on his armor and to ensure that the knightly swords as well as other arms were polished until they shone. Meanwhile, he would stand by to attend to his knight in battle. His master acted as a tutor and taught William all he needed to know to become a knight.

Much to Hilda's dismay, when Henry and then John reached the age of seven, Roger sent them away to train as knights too. She pled with Roger, "Please, we only have three sons. Can't one stay home with me?"

"What! And you would spoil him like you do me? No, my lovely. I want all your attention." Then he patted her on her cheek.

Scowling at him, she stomped her foot and shook her long blonde hair. "Oh, you make me so angry at times that I wonder why I love you."

"Because I love you better than anyone else ever can," he retorted.

At times, Roger, who had great judgment and military skill, was called upon to support the King. The other courtiers were not pleased when that occurred. They envied Roger because the King listened to him and heeded his counsel. They would glower and mutter to each other when Roger was in attendance upon the King. Later, when the King would quote Roger and say, "Roger said..." and "Roger told me," the knights would scowl.

When the King called for him, Roger would gather up his squire and the lesser knights in the region. He would hold a great, six-course banquet in his hall and serve people from the finest plates of gold and silver. Then he would bid farewell to his beautiful wife and ride off into the sunset, leading his army. When he returned, there would be another great banquet, music and dancing.

When William, Henry and John reached the age of twenty-one, they were each made knights. In an elaborate ceremony, they were admonished to protect the weak, to right wrongs and to honor women. After their armor was buckled on, piece by piece, they were dubbed knights.

Hilda was proud of each of her sons, but she found that they often ignored her. They rode their horses, practiced their swordplay, discussed siege warfare and weapons with their father and yawned loudly when she discussed poetry and courtly love. Sometimes Hilda found herself most vexed with them.

William, Henry and John were knights now. Often they went riding forth in quest of adventure, clad in armor and with sword, shield, and lance ready to hand. As knight-errants, they sought fair maidens in need of a champion or strange knights with whom to joust. Sometimes one or two of the brothers would station themselves at a crossroad to challenge any other knight who traveled the road. Attractive young men, they were usually sure of hospitality at any castle to which they visited. Occasionally, they would return to their parents' castle while they waited for the call for crusaders to rescue the Holy Sepulcher. They had great visions of pursuing and killing the Saracens and capturing Jerusalem.

When they came home, they would greet their mother and then ignore her. She admonished them, saying, "A knight should be bold, fair, courteous and generous. He should be proud and fierce to his enemies, and kind to his friends."

"But we are, mother. We just don't want to talk about courtly love. Have you heard about these new longbows? They're really going to change the way we fight."

Sometimes Hilda wished she hadn't stopped having children. A girl might be more understanding of her needs, she thought.

She commented to her husband that their sons lacked common courtesy. "They don't even say please or thank you—no matter what I do for them."

"They are young. Customs have changed. Everything is changing—now there's this new crossbow."

"They don't ask for help very nicely," she sniffed.

"I expect you want them to be the truly perfect gentle knights."

"Yes, I expect I do. Good knights have courtesy after all."

"Hmm," Roger stroked his beard. He knew she was right, but he didn't want to admit it.

Roger had been quite successful over the years. He had a nice castle and many loyal vassals and peasants. He had established a powerful dynasty with three robust sons. He and Hilda had celebrated their golden wedding anniversary, which was a milestone in those days when people certainly did not live as long as they do now. And he had collected a small fortune, which he kept carefully hidden in an old chest.

One day one of Roger's former squires rode into the courtyard saying that some of the courtiers had secretly persuaded the King to arrest Roger on the charge of treason and to obtain forfeiture of his castle and his estate for the King's security. Knowing that his family would lose his fortune, if he were found guilty, Roger hugged his Hilda, told her that he loved her and carefully wrapped a large chain around his treasure chest. Then he put on his armor and got on his horse while carrying the chest. He went into a heavily wooded region where few birds sang and the sun was reduced to pale shafts of light. Deep in the woods was a well, where Roger dropped his chest.

Once Roger concealed his treasure, he hid in the branches of a great oak that stood in the proximity of the well and watched for his enemies. One night, however, he fell asleep and fell into the well, where he drowned. Even a good man like Roger couldn't swim when wearing armor.

Meanwhile, his wife and sons waited for him to return home. The King who had threatened to put him in the Tower was dead, and a new King, with far greater problems than Roger, sat on the throne. Roger's possible treason was no longer a concern.

Hilda was sure that Roger was dead. Their love was too great for him to abandon her in this manner. Sniffling quietly, she mourned him, but as the months went on she mourned the loss of the treasure more. Life was not as good without

Roger's careful land management and care for the estate. Finally, she decided to send William to the well.

When William arrived at that dark dank place, he saw a specter, clad in shining armor, glaring at him. William was too scared to go further. He came home and told his mother. Unfortunately, he also told his betrothed who told her parents that a ghost had scared her strong stalwart William. They told their friends, who told theirs, and when William returned everyone laughed and mocked him. No longer was the court a good place for him.

Hilda sent her second son, Henry, to fetch the treasure. He avoided looking at the man in armor, hauled the chest to the brink of the well, but then the chain snapped. For thirty days, he hauled up the chest and for thirty days the chain snapped. Meanwhile, the specter watched. Henry thought the specter even laughed once. Finally, he returned home empty-handed.

John, the third son, traveled to the dark moldy woods. Just as he began to feel foolish and wondered what his wife would say, the armored specter loomed over him. John quickly grabbed the chain, dragging the chest to the top of the well, but then it fell back, bringing him with it. Unfortunately, no one heard his shouts so he drowned.

Seeing the dismal failure of her three sons, Hilda decided she would go herself. When she got to the wooded area, she saw the armored specter standing there. Her heart pounding, she stood there. The specter came closer. She drew back because the specter smelled of mold and wet dank earth. She said, "Roger, I need your help. Please give me the treasure." She thought the specter was trying to speak from his fearsome grimaces, but she heard no words. "Help me, Roger, please," she urged. The specter nodded, pulled up the chest, opened it, and gave its contents to her.

When she arrived home with the treasure, her two remaining sons were astounded. "Mother, how did you ever manage to get your hands on Father's treasure," asked William.

"I just said please," she replied, smiling sweetly.

# The Cripplegate Ghost

Once upon a time, there was a beautiful woman with copper-colored hair, who loved living in London. She liked the theaters and the cockfights, Hyde Park and Birdcage Walk – the goings-on of a big busy city that had welcomed back the dashing young King Charles II. She often stayed out later than she should and slept late during the day while her husband worked to support her. Held close in her husband's arms, she felt happy, but she found watching London at play to be more exciting than being in bed with her husband. So she gallivanted, while he worked to support them.

Maybe she got a disease or fell down the stairs or perhaps she partied too much. Some say she had catalepsy. Anyway, she fell into a coma. When three weeks had passed, the doctor pronounced her dead – much to her husband's dismay. So he had her beautiful body wrapped in a winding sheet, placed in a coffin and buried in the graveyard of St. Giles of Cripplegate. Her husband sat by her grave mourning for several hours and then went home to his empty house filled with her furbelows and the heavy musky perfume with which she always surrounded herself.

Now, the church sexton knew that the beautiful young woman had been buried with a large emerald on the fourth finger of her left hand. He was a short man with a head too large for his narrow shoulders and a narrow-nosed, tight-lipped face. His eyes were hard and cold, and he too adored his wife. He said to her, "Look, wife, the woman we buried today had a large emerald on her finger. What would you think about us going to the graveyard tonight, digging up her coffin and grabbing the ring?"

"I think that's a wonderful idea, dear husband." His plump wife had badly pockmarked skin, although she covered it with a thick layer of cosmetics. She admitted to thirty-two of her forty-eight years and spent a good deal of time contriving to look younger than she was. An emerald ring, she thought, would be just perfect. Her only problem would be whether to keep it, wearing it on the fourth finger of her large reddened hand, or to pawn it so she could increase her spending power.

That night the couple went to the graveyard, dug up the coffin and lifted the heavy lid. The dead woman's slim hands were folded across her chest. The emerald ring surrounded by diamonds glittered in the moonlight. The woman could feel her face flush with excitement. "It's beautiful, my beloved. I must have it." She eagerly grabbed the woman's slim white hand and pulled at the ring, but it wouldn't come off. "Funny," she thought. "Her finger doesn't look that big." She spat on the finger, hoping that her salvia would ease the ring's exit from the finger, but that didn't work either. "I can't get the ring off," she gasped.

"Of course, you can," replied her husband.

"I tell you I can't," she screamed.

The sexton turned around with his eyes snapping dangerously. "You fool. Learn to govern your tongue. People may be in earshot."

Not wanting to be arrested for robbing the dead, his wife said more calmly. "I can't get the ring off her finger. You try."

"Give it here." He pulled the ring, but it remained stuck. He pulled again, yanking so hard that the body of the woman began to sit up.

"Cut off her finger with your knife, husband."

As he pulled his knife out of his belt and reached for the slim white finger, the dead woman sat up all the way. The sexton's wife backed away, gasping. "She's come back from the dead."

"Maybe this is her ghost. Run!" Off they went.

Wrapped in her winding sheet, the beautiful woman got out of the coffin and began walking to her home in Cripplegate. She could barely hear the bellman's monotonous "Past one o'clock of a cold autumn night." There were no streetlights – only the pale glow from the new moon. The streets appeared to be empty, but she knew that the London streets were never empty and often dangerous. She took great care in walking home because she had just escaped being buried alive and losing her fourth finger on her left hand. Her shoes were soaked through by the time the moon was fading. When she knocked on her front door, her servant approached and asked, "Who's there?"

"It is I. Your mistress. Let me in for I am freezing."

The servant ran to tell her master that the ghost of his wife was at the door. A sensible man, he let in his shivering wife, who obviously wasn't a ghost. Then he swung her up off the floor, kissing her face again and again. "Oh, I'm so glad to see you back from the dead."

"And I you." She kept stroking his cheeks, running her hands over his back. She realized she had missed the feeling of warmth and happiness he brought into a room with him; she had missed the evenings when they played cribbage and he had listened to her sing. She missed his smile and the sound of his voice. He called for hot drinks and a bed warmer to be placed in their bed.

In the ensuing years, she bore three children, who were fascinated by her story of being buried alive. She learned how to make bread and keep house. When she died at a good old age, she was buried with her ring in the Cripplegate Parish Church yard. Her story of being rescued from the grave was inscribed on her tombstone.

# Bleeding Heart Yard

*Of poor Lady Hatton, it's needless to say,*
*No traces have ever been found to this day,*
*Or the terrible dancer who whisk'd her away;*
*But out in the courtyard — and just in that part*
*Where the pump stands —*
*lay bleeding a* LARGE HUMAN HEART*!*
R.H. Barham. *The Ingoldsby Legends*

According to legend, the courtyard is named Bleeding Heart Yard to commemorate the murder of Lady Elizabeth Hatton, a daughter of Sir Christopher Hatton, a prominent Royalist during the reign of King Charles I of England. After the Restoration, he was made a privy counselor and governor of Guernsey. He is buried in Westminister Abbey.

In one story, his gorgeous daughter Elizabeth, who was always wanting something better than her lot in life, made a contract with the devil in exchange for wealth, status and a mansion in Holburn in Central London. She spent the evening of January 26 with the Bishop of Ely at an extravagant ball in Hatton House. During the dance, she danced with the devil. Then she disappeared. Later, her body was found, appearing as if it had been "torn limb from limb." A passerby found her still beating heart in the courtyard the next morning in what is now called Bleeding Heart Yard.

In the Charles Dickens novel, *Little Dorritt*, Bleeding Heart Yard is the home of the Plornish family.

*[It was] a place much changed in feature and in fortune, yet with some relish of ancient greatness about it. Two or three mighty stacks*

Bleeding Heart Yard now has a wonderful pub.
*Courtesy of D. Peter Lund*

*of chimneys, and a few large dark rooms which had escaped being walled and subdivided out of the recognition of their old proportions, gave the Yard a character. It was inhabited by poor people, who set up their rest among its faded glories, as Arabs of the desert pitch their tents among the fallen stones of the Pyramids; but there was a family sentimental feeling prevalent in the Yard, that it had a character.*

**Directions:** Exit Farringdon Station, go straight ahead to Cowcross Street. Go straight, crossing Farrington Road on to Greville Street, Bleeding Heart Yard is a cobbled street on the left.

# The Merry Monarch and Some of His Women

The Restoration transformed the English court from the Scripture-loving Puritan regime of Oliver Cromwell and his followers (1649-1660) to the glittering center of English society and the merry rule of Charles II. England had called Charles Stuart back to his kingdom after years of Puritanical sobriety. The great palace at Whitehall, with its 1,400 rooms and lavish decoration, was once again full of the beautiful people of the day, ranging from painted ladies, to ambassadors, to fawning toadies. Now, they could trade in their black unadorned clothes for curls, ribbons, flounces and feathers. Men replaced the broad, high-waisted silhouette of the previous period with a long, lean line with a low waist and donned wigs with flowing shoulder-length curls. Women had ringlets and low broad necklines, displayed their petticoats, and wore tight corsets to highlight their tiny waists.

Women played a prominent role in Charles II's life. While he was still in exile, Lucy Walters bore him a son, James, whom he later created Duke of Monmouth. The promiscuous Barbara Palmer, Lady Castlemaine, was already his mistress, although married to the poor Roger Palmer, when Charles wed shy Catharine of Braganza. Charles and Catherine never had any children, but he certainly wasn't childless. Eventually, he had over a dozen children by several mistresses – just none by his own wife!

Poor Catherine. Back in Portugal, her mother had warned her about Lady Castlemaine and told her never to allow that woman's name to be mentioned in her presence or to allow her in court. The greedy Lady Castlemaine certainly wouldn't accept back street status, and Charles didn't know how to draw the line, so eventually Catherine had to give in. Over the years,

Lady Castlemaine had six children, and Charles acknowledged five of them. Hard to swallow if you are a barren Queen.

One of the great amusements at the Restoration court was watching Charles play his women one against the other. Women besieged him. Some newspapers even ran cartoons of him, being pursued by women as he ran, clinging to his crown. Charles didn't get rid of his mistresses. Although he might tire of them, he kept them "on the string," so to speak! His courtiers said of him, "His Majesty never discards; he adds to his hand."

Happily immoral, Charles was not devoted to any one woman. Catherine had to put up with his mistresses and his illegitimate children – many of whom were created dukes! Referring to Charles II "as the father of his people," the Duke of Buckingham wryly commented after a pregnant pause, "of a good many of them."

This new era was one of sexual adventure when maidens were told to gather their roses, the plays were bawdy, and pleasure was key. Charles liked an attractive face and a pretty figure, and he found the stage a handy hunting ground. Like many others, he chose his mistresses from the ranks of the new professionals – much to the dismay of his Queen and Lady Castlemaine.

In 1667, Moll Davis, a popular singer-dancer-comedienne became one of Charles' mistresses. Much to the envy of others, Moll paraded her 'mighty pretty fine coach' and an expensive ring. One of her fellow actresses, Nell Gwyn, once an orange seller in the theater, and her gentleman friend were at the Lincoln's Inn Fields' theater. In the next box was Charles II, who preferred to flirt with the cute cockney actress, whom Pepys later referred to as 'pretty, witty Nell,' than to follow the play. Charles and his brother James (the future James II) invited the seventeen-year-old Nell and her friend to supper. Supposedly, the royal brothers discovered that they had no money to pay the bill. "Od's fish!" Nell exclaimed, mimicking the King's speech, "but this is the poorest company I ever was in!"

A true child of the streets, Nell was born in London's East End in 1650; her father disappeared when she was born, her mother kept a brothel at Covent Garden. Once she sold oranges at the theater, but then a lover taught her how to act. Before long, she was appearing in Restoration plays and winning the hearts of growing audiences. Incidentally, Nell was so illiterate so the only way she could memorize her lines was having them read to her. As one of Charles' mistresses, however, she was no longer Mrs. Nell Gwyn, the actress. Her life changed overnight.

Nell, who retained the King's affections as much by her wits as her looks, enjoyed the good life. Historians have found that the self-proclaimed "Protestant whore," spent lavishly. Now, she traveled everywhere by sedan chair. A shop alcoholic, she ordered a silver bed that cost £150,000 (at today's values), purchased three barrels of oysters a week, ordered children's gloves at a shilling each by the dozen and billed the Royal Treasury for her rum, brandy, cheese and even fruit. Obviously, she kept meticulous records.

Charles was not known for his faithfulness; consequently, Nell had her rivals. She succeeded in maintaining her relationship with Charles through her optimism and humor. Learning that Moll was supposed to sleep with the King one night, Nell invited her to eat some laxative-filled teacakes. Although Moll enjoyed the teacakes, they had their repercussions, ruining the night in the royal bed. Retiring from her stage life in 1668, Moll bore Charles a daughter in 1669. The King gave her a house and a pension.

Another of Nell's competitors was the Catholic Louise de Keroualle from France. Arriving in London from Versailles, Louise looked askance at Nell and her jokes. Nell called her "weeping willow," because Louise used tears to obtain gifts and favors from Charles. She also referred to Louise as Squintabella because she had a slight cast in one eye. Charles considered both nicknames hilarious; Louise was not amused and berated him for being involved with this coarse, common "orange wench."

Nell Gwyn, an English comedienne and mistress of Charles II, epitomizes the fun-loving spirit of Restoration England. She rose from dire poverty to become one of Charles' most beloved mistresses. The English people love Nell, who made it to the top. This picture of her was on the wall of a tube station. *Courtesy of D. Peter Lund*

Nell's sense of humor endeared her to London citizens. One day, she was passing through the streets of Oxford, in her coach, when an angry mob assumed she was her rival, Louise, known as the *Catholic whore.* The people on the street began verbally abusing her and shouting "No Popery!" Sticking her head out of the coach window, "Good people," she said, smiling, "you are mistaken; I am the *Protestant* whore."

Several stories are told about how Nell's oldest (Charles' seventh son by the way) was given the Earldom of Burford. The most popular is that when her son Charles was six years old, Nell said, "Come here, you little bastard, and say hello to your father," when his father came calling. When the King admonished her for calling his son a bastard, she replied, "Your Majesty has given me no other name by which to call him." Consequently, Charles made him the Earl of Burford. Dukedoms were not easy to come by — especially when the King had so many natural sons. Another story is that Nell grabbed young Charles and hung him out of a window (or over a river) and threatened to drop him unless the King granted him a peerage. The King cried out, "God save the Earl of Burford!"

On his deathbed in 1685, the King begged his brother and successor, James "Do not let poor Nelly starve." James generously paid Nell's debts, saving her from Newgate prison, and gave her a country estate in Nottingham. Nell died two years after Charles at the age of 37.

Unlike Charles' other mistresses, Nell was more concerned about the welfare of others. After happening upon an old soldier begging in the street, she persuaded the King to build the Royal Hospital in Chelsea for ex-servicemen. Today it is the home of the red-coated Chelsea Pensioners. In her will she "laid out £20 yearly for the releasing of poor debtors from prison," a fate she had escaped through her own high spirits and the love of Charles II.

### Children of Charles II

Charles II awarded dukedoms to six of his illegitimate sons. Four dukedoms still survive. His daughters generally married nobility.

Diana, Princess of Wales, was descended from two of Charles's illegitimate sons, the Duke of Grafton and the Duke of Richmond (who is also a direct ancestor of Camilla, Duchess of Cornwall, second wife of Charles, Prince of Wales). Diana and Charles' son, Prince William of Wales, second in line to the British throne, is likely to be the first monarch descended from Charles II.

# The Law Student

It was a narrow, dirty, disreputable alley. The houses were crazily built; their overhanging stories leaned across the street almost touching at the top and blocking light and air from the piles of filth that lay below in the alley. Perceval's body was lying in the filth of the gutter. They called me.

When I inspected his body, I found that he had been run through with his own sword. He had terrible gaping wounds about the face and the chest. According to the papers in his pocket, he was a student at Lincoln's Inn. For those of you who don't know, every English barrister belongs to one of the Inns of Court in London. It is like a professional association, with supervisory and disciplinary functions over their members. The Inns also provide libraries, dining facilities and professional accommodation.

I asked around at the Inns and received strange looks and sniggering remarks. When I pieced it all together, I discovered that Perceval is what twenty-first century police would call a punk. Here, he was a cousin of Prime Minister Spencer, a British statesman who served George III, yet he led a life of debauchery. He gambled. He consorted with prostitutes. He borrowed money from his friends and didn't pay them back. He cheated at cards. He certainly didn't concentrate on his legal studies.

I asked to speak to one of Percevel's friends. Perhaps he could give me more information about this young man who had reached this unfortunate end. A Cecil Castle came forward. A thin young man with shrewd blue eyes, he said to me, "You are not going to believe my story. I'm not sure that I believe my story, but this is what Perceval told me one night when he had imbibed too much brandy."

"I gather he often did that."

"True, but he rarely talked about his feelings. He was a man who would not be tied or bound or obligated. His ideal was to do as he wished when he wished."

I said, "Young man. Thank you for coming forth. Pray be seated. Why don't you tell me your story? You look like a trustworthy individual." I hesitated and then added with a warning smile, "After all, you are studying to be a barrister."

"Yes, sir." He sat down, and I sat across from him. "Perceval told me that one night he was studying late in his chambers. His room – like most of our rooms – was small, bare and dark. It was furnished with some worn cane-bottomed stools and chairs, and his table was piled high with books. Of course, Perceval rarely opened them – he was too preoccupied with other activities." The young man laughed cynically.

"Yes, I know. The nefarious type of activities."

"Yes. Anyway, Perceval was studying that night, which is quite remarkable. He very rarely opened a book. Outside, the moonless night was frosty. He told me the clock had just struck midnight when he felt a cold draft and chills go up his spine. Turning, he saw a misty figure wrapped in a winding sheet that covered his face. Perceval knew he had locked his door. He jumped up from his chair, demanding, 'Who are you? How did you get in?' There was no answer. The specter came closer.

In the center of London lies Lincoln's Inn with its ancient halls.

"What do you want?" he asked. Still no answer.

The specter came closer. The closer the specter came, the more frightened Perceval became. He shouted again, 'Tell me your name or else I will slay you.'

"The specter still did not reply. So Perceval picked up his sword and swung at the mysterious specter, only to see his blade pass right through its neck. Terrified, he leapt at the figure and unwrapped its face. Staring at him was his own face but with terrible gaping wounds about it and the chest. Perceval told me he was so frightened that he screamed."

"What happened then?"

"The specter disappeared. Perceval said it was like he evaporated. Certainly, he didn't go through the door."

"Do you think he was fabricating the truth?" I asked.

"Honestly? No, I don't. He appeared to be really terrified. He was shaking as he told me the story."

"So what happened after that?" I asked.

"During the next several weeks, much to my amazement, Perceval made an about face. He decided to reform his way of living. He gave up the gambling and the women and began to study. He did well. His instructors were surprised at his prowess. His more dissolute friends ignored him because he was no longer ready to gamble for high stakes or to go out on the town. His family began to speak to him again. He started talking about what he would do in the future: a job, a wife..."

Perceval's friend sighed. "But one moonless night, he told me he couldn't stand being so good. That it was too dull. So he went out that night."

**Directions:** Take the northbound Victoria Line and change at Oxford Circus taking the Central Line to Holborn Underground Station. Turn left out of the station on to Kingsway, continue down the left hand side of this street for about five minutes until you reach Sardinia Street. Turn left into Sardinia Street to enter Lincoln's Inn Fields.

# Royal London Parks

The Green Park lies between Hyde Park and St. James's Park. Charles II laid out the park's main walks and built an icehouse there to supply ice for cooling drinks in summer. At this time, the park was in an outlying area of London. It was not until the mid-eighteenth century that it was safe from highwaymen and thieves. Nearby lies the beautiful St. James's Park. Originally laid out for James I in 1603, Charles II had it re-landscaped in 1660. In 1667, he introduced exotic birds to the park.

If you walk on the path through the park, you come to a small lake, which is spanned by a bridge. Some say that they have seen a headless woman in this area. She slowly emerges from the placid lake waters and walks across its surface to land. There, she runs frantically towards the bushes, where she disappears.

People believe she is the wife of a sergeant in the guard who murdered her in the 1780s. Hacking off her head, he buried it before flinging her body into the marsh. Since that fateful day, the headless woman searches in vain for her missing head.

Today, the park is wooded meadows. Originally, it was a swampy burial ground for lepers from the nearby hospital at St James', which is said to be the reason for its lack of flowers.

The Crusades are though to have introduced leprosy into England. During the thirteenth century, lepers were segregated from the rest of society. To warn of their approach, they carried a bell or clapper. Leper hospitals were a prominent feature of medieval life. There were over 200 hospitals run along monastic lines in England. Lepers were encouraged to live in these monastic-type establishments for their own health as well as quarantine. Some medieval sources believe

Londoners talk about the Tree of Death. *Courtesy of D. Peter Lund*

that those suffering from leprosy were considered to be going through Purgatory on Earth. For this reason, their suffering was considered more holy than the ordinary person's.

Workers talk quietly about a particular tree in the park, which emits a general feeling of melancholy. No birds sing from its branches, and dogs avoid it. Calling it the 'Tree of Death,' they give it a wide berth when working in the park. Supposedly, people have committed suicide from its branches. Some have heard the tree utter a throaty, gurgling chuckle. Others have glimpsed a tall, shadowy figure that stands beside the tree, pointing at them, but which vanishes the moment any brave or curious person moves towards it.

**Directions:** Exit St. James Park Station, cross Old Queen Street, turn left on Birdcage Walk and cross to St. James Park.

# The Most Haunted House

For more than fifty years, Maggs Bros, Antiquarian Booksellers, have occupied 50 Berkeley Square, a four-story townhouse dating back to the 1740s. They have lined the downstairs with high mahogany bookcases that contain many shelves of leather-bound books. The Georgian building has sweeping stairs, marble floors, fireplaces, and high ceilings. It doesn't look like a building that would attract ghosts, yet it does.

This house has the reputation for being the most haunted house in London – which says a lot, given how many ghosts seem to wander about the city. Either the booksellers who occupy it now have a great press agent or it really is haunted!

During the first half of the nineteenth century, the house was often empty and deserted for great stretches of time. In 1840, people heard "supernatural" noises coming from it. One person insisted that a little Scots girl dressed in a kilt haunted the house. The child was supposed to have been tortured to death in the top-most room of the house. Another says a young woman called Adeline lived at the house with her lecherous uncle. To escape him, Adeline climbed out of a top floor window and fell to the ground. Since then, people have seen her on the top floor, sobbing and wringing her hands in despair.

In the 1850s, a maid stayed in the haunted room overnight. Her screams awoke the owners downstairs. Going to her room, they found her lying on the bed, her face hideously twisted, her eyes fixed, staring in terror. She died in hospital the next day, never describing what she had seen.

Many would-be ghost-busters have tried to sleep in the house. One young man said that he did not believe in ghosts and haunted rooms. "Unadulterated poppycock," he declared. He made a bet that he could spend a night in the haunted room. He arranged for a bell to be rigged up in the room so that he could call for help if he needed it. "If I ring once," said he, "take no notice, for I might be only nervous, without due course; but if I ring twice come to me." With his friends sleeping downstairs, he went to bed in the haunted room, holding a gun for protection. At 2 am, his friends heard his bell ringing. As they ran upstairs, a gunshot rang out. On entering the room, they found the young man dead. He was lying against the wall, his eyes wide and his face contorted in fear—without a mark on him. The smoking gun was in his hand and a bullet hole was in the wall.

Maggs Bros. Ltd., established in 1853, is one of the world's largest antiquarian booksellers. *Courtesy of D. Peter Lund*

During the 1870s, the neighbors reported hearing screams and loud cries coming from the locked and vacant house at night. They also heard the sound of furniture being dragged across the floor, bells ringing and windows being slammed shut. Although the house was deserted, furniture and books were thrown out the windows onto the street below.

Years later the house was occupied by a Mr. Dupre, who locked his insane brother in a room on the top floor. He made a special opening in the door so he could feed his brother. Supposedly, that is when the room acquired its name as the Haunted Room. By 1872, no one would live in the house. A Lord Lyttleton decided, on a dare, to spend a night in the haunted room. He took a shotgun and, when something jumped out at him at night, he fired it. When he turned on the light, nothing was there of course.

On Christmas Eve, 1887, according to sailor Robert Martin, he and Edward Blunden needed a place to spend the night. "So we found the empty house in Berkeley Square and decided to sleep there. Yes, I know it was breaking in, but we didn't want to sleep on the street. We slept in the room at the top of the house. I found out much later that it is called the haunted room. Now I know why.

"During the night, we heard these shuffling footsteps coming up the stairs and smelled a bad aroma. The door creaked open, and something entered the bedroom. I saw it seize Ed by the throat. His legs were flailing, and he was making this awful noise. I was trembling. My teeth were chattering so loud that I could hear them. I managed to rush past it, leaving poor old Ed, and raced down the stairs to go get help.

"I found some police and when we went back, we found Ed stone cold dead. He had been strangled. The police found nothing."

In the 1900s, according to the story, an elderly couple acted as caretakers for the house, but they were never allowed to enter the haunted room, which was locked. Every six months, a man called and spent several hours in the room after having first locked the couple in the basement.

Today, the employees of Maggs Bookshop report strange happenings. One saw a mass of brown mist (could that be the shapeless slithering mass) move quickly across the room and then vanish. A cleaning lady felt the presence of someone following her around the house. A man was walking upstairs when his glasses were torn off his face and thrown across the room.

Employees are not allowed to go up to the top floor. They say that there's a police notice hanging on the wall inside the house that was put up in the 1950s. It states that the top floor of the house is not to be used, even for storage.

**Directions:** From the Green Park Station, take Queens Walk to Piccadilly Street. Cross over to Berkeley Street and walk down that until you come to Berkeley Square. Walk around until you come to #50.

# LORE

Then there are those tales that are part of our history. They are ones we all know — that we have grown up with — where the spirits from the past remain with us today.

# El Draque

*Sometimes when we can't understand why we are not winning, we attribute our loss to the other's power. The superstitious Spanish attributed Sir Francis Drake's seafaring victories to his pact with the Powers of Darkness. They saw no other way that a heretic Englishman could repeatedly outwit their admirals and grand sailing fleet and bring havoc to their ports. They called him El Draque, a name used to frighten recalcitrant children. They believed that the devil showed him the enemy fleets and their proposed strategies in a magic mirror. The devil also gave him the ability "to garner the winds and to loose or bind them at his will."*

*Drake's Devon countrymen looked upon him as a magician, capable of using white magic. But perhaps the Spanish were more correct... While Drake was in the Antipodes, they said that he drew upon his magic mirror to see that his wife, believing him dead, was about to marry again. To prevent the marriage, he fired a cannon through the globe so that the shot burst through the earth between her and her fiancé. She said, "That's Drake," and canceled the ceremony.*

After the horrors of Smithfield and the enforced return to Catholicism during the reign of Queen Mary, England reveled in Elizabeth I. She led England to what is known as the Golden Age. During her reign, from November 17, 1558, to March 24,1603, English explorers such as Sir Francis Drake and Sir Walter Raleigh expanded English territory and trade overseas until England became a major force on the world stage.

## The Seaman

Francis Drake was the son of a fervent Protestant, who supposedly resided in one of the abandoned warships left from Henry VIII's efforts to build a navy a decade earlier. His father apprenticed him to a small coastal vessel that sailed from port to port in the North Sea, a harsh stretch of water.

Francis learned his seafaring craft well, and his master left him the little ship. He did well, but he soon became bored.

Ambitious and with a desire for adventure, he sold his ship and joined the fleet owned by his cousin John Hawkins. Despite the huge wealth flowing into Spain and the Spanish presence in the Americas, much remained to be discovered and exploited. During this time, Drake formed a hatred for the Spanish, which led to his lifelong revenge against them. Drake raided Spanish harbors, captured and looted Spanish ships, and stole gold, silver and gems. Previously, an unknown lad from Devonshire, England, he became a swashbuckling hero.

Queen Elizabeth was delighted with Drake's exploits and the treasure he brought home. England was now on friendly terms with Spain, however, so Drake needed to disappear and not play the hero. For three years, he served the Queen in Ireland, where he dreamed about destroying the Spanish monopoly of the Pacific, conducting raids on the colonies along the west coast of South America, and perhaps even founding English colonies in the New World.

When relations between England and Spain deteriorated, the Queen invited him to an audience. She agreed to support secretly Drake's piracy against Spain so that King Philip's treasure might find its way into her coffers. Financed by Elizabeth and her most prominent noblemen, Drake charted a voyage that was to sail around the world.

The expedition, consisting of a fleet of five ships, set sail from Plymouth Sound in Devon, England, in 1577. The historic voyage was approximately thirty-six thousand miles. Drake navigated his way through the Strait of Magellan, pressed north to Chile and Peru, where he plundered Spanish ships of their gold and silver treasure. In his wake, the Spaniards spread tales of the English pirate, "El Draque." He made a landing in 1579 at or near Drake's Bay, California, and arrived home in 1580, laden with captured Spanish treasure and a cargo of spices. The *Golden Hind** was the only ship out of the original fleet of five to have returned. The Queen's half-share of the cargo surpassed the rest of her income for that entire year. Hailing Drake as the first Englishman (Magellan had sailed it in 1519) to circumnavigate the globe, Queen Elizabeth knighted him aboard the *Golden Hind* on April 4, 1581.

In 1585, war broke out between Spain and England over religious and commercial differences. Drake managed to delay the Spanish invasion for one year by conducting many daring raids of the Armada's ships and stores. He sailed to the New World and captured the Spanish port towns, Santo Domingo and Cartagena, and held them for ransom. On his way home to England, he destroyed the Spanish settlement at St. Augustine in Florida. Then, to add fuel to the fire, Drake "singed the beard of the King of Spain" by sailing a fleet into Cadiz, Spain, occupying the harbor and destroying thirty-seven naval and merchant ships.

Sir Francis Drake sailed The *Golden Hind* around the world between 1577 and 1580. *Courtesy of D. Peter Lund*

He then occupied the town of Sagres and seized a large Portuguese carrack laden with a rich cargo.

In 1588, King Phillip II of Spain resolved to invade England. A huge fleet of Spanish and Portuguese ships was amassed, and thousands of soldiers were sent to Flanders to prepare for an invasion. When the massive Spanish Armada slowly sailed up the English Channel, Lord Admiral Charles Howard and Vice-Admiral Drake stood back and watched the Spanish galleons with their high turrets. According to one legend, Drake calmly continued with his game of bowls, saying, "There is plenty of time to finish the game and beat the Spaniards too." That night Drake pursued one galleon, which surrendered to him when its captain learned that his attacker was the fearsome El Draque.

Ashore, series of hillside bonfires spread the news of the Armada's sighting, and the militia rallied to defend the country. This network of "fires over England" still takes place today to celebrate coronations and royal jubilees. Supposedly, the fifty-four year old Queen traveled to inspect the militia in Tilbury as they prepared for the invasion force. There, she gave one of her famous speeches:

> *I am come amongst you, as you see...in the midst and heat of the battle to live and die amongst you all.... I have the body of a weak and feeble woman, but I have the heart and stomach of a king.*

The English commanders decided to let the Armada pass and to pursue it up the Channel. Several nights later, the English dispatched deadly fire ships into the enemy's fleet as it lay at anchor. "Devil ships" whispered the terrified Spanish sailors. In the resulting confusion, the remains of the Spanish army fled into the open sea. The following day at the Battle of Gravelines, the great Armada was beaten. Nearly half the Spanish ships never returned home. As many as nine thousand men were lost, and those who survived were starving. Many ended up in Ireland, and Spanish wrecks are said to lie off Ireland's west coast. By contrast, not one English ship was lost during the engagement. The great victory was celebrated across the country.

Drake continued his seafaring career into his mid-fifties. In 1595, he suffered several defeats in Spanish America. In 1596, at the age of 56, he died of dysentery, while anchored off the coast of Panama where some Spanish treasure ships had sought shelter. He was buried at sea in a lead coffin.

### The Wizard

Drake's adventures have become a part of the world's folklore. Most of us have heard of the fireships and the Spanish Armada. Numerous stories and fictional adaptations of his adventures exist to this day.

The Spanish believed that the devil helped Drake on sea and in battle. Those who live in the West Country of England say that on stormy nights his ghost drives a hearse, drawn by headless horses and followed by headless hounds. In the 1830s, they said when the Armada threatened that Drake took his stand by the seashore with a block of wood and an axe. As the wood chips flew into the water, each chip became a fire ship that hassled the Spanish. He is said to have developed a new source of pure water from Dartmoor to Plymouth and to have built a barn with the devil's help.

A stirring poem written by Henry Newbolt in 1895 is the basis of the legend of Drake as the guardian of England and of the drum as the instrument used to call for his help. The poem says that when Drake lay dying he commanded that his drum should be returned to England and promised that if it were struck when invasion was threatened, he would return to drive off the enemy. Later, the story was altered to say that the drum would call for him on its own accord.

> *Take my drum to England, hang et by the shore,*
> *Strike et when your powder's runnin' low;*
> *If the Dons sight Devon, I'll quit the port o' Heaven,*
> *An' drum them up the Channel as we drummed them long ago.*
> Sir Henry Newbolt, *Drake's Drum*

People claim the drum has been heard at times when England is at war or a significant national event takes place. For example, it beat during the Dunkirk evacuation in 1940, and the Falklands War in 1982. The drum is currently located in the Drake, Naval and West Country Folk Museum at Buckland Abbey, Devon, England.

* Drake renamed his ship *Pelican* in 1577, as he prepared to enter the Strait of Magellan. He called it *Golden Hind* to compliment his patron, Sir Christopher Hatton, whose armorial crest (family coat of arms) was a golden 'hind' (the heraldic term for a female deer). Hatton was one of the principal sponsors of Drake's world voyage.

**Directions:** Today, a full-size replica of the *Golden Hinde* is berthed at St. Mary Overie Dock in Southwark, London, between Southwark Cathedral and Clink Street. It was launched in 1973. Public tours are available. Go across London Bridge until you reach Borough High Street. Turn right on Cathedral Street, which brings you to the replica of the *Golden Hind.*

# Wizard of the Seas

Pirates have been around for a long time. The Vikings could even be considered pirates since they attacked ships and ports. Many pirates were outlaws, but, thanks to Hollywood, many of us think of pirates as the dashing, well-educated sons of upright families. We view them as the swashbuckling Robin Hoods of the sea, sporting cocked pistols, eye patches, and cutlasses. They know how to swashbuckle, mop the poop deck, use a cat o'nine tails, and – if they must – walk the plank. Some like John Hawkins profited royally from stealing slaves from Portuguese ships off West Africa and selling them illegally all over the Spanish Main. Some like English-born Blackbeard chose piracy over unemployment at the end of one of the many European wars. Others were like Stede Bonnet, who had retired from the Army, owned a large property in Barbados and lived in a fine house with his wife. His neighbors understood that because his wife harassed him so much, he had become unbalanced mentally and had taken to piracy.

Of course, avarice was the great culprit. The great riches of the Spanish Main were what lured so many seafarers into the life of a pirate. From the sixteenth to the eighteenth century, the Spanish fleet would transport great hoards of gold, silver, gems, spices, hardwoods, leather, and other riches from the New World to Spain. Although buccaneers are supposed to have wooden sea chests loaded with gold bullion, pieces of eight, and jewels, their treasure was more often hogsheads of sugar, pewter, silverware, bolts of cloth, and other practical necessities from captured merchant ships. The pirate captain sometimes took the whole ship as a prize and forced the captive crew to join him.

Old Bailey is England's Central Criminal Court, which deals with major criminal cases from Greater London and from other parts of England. Built on the site of the Newgate Prison, the present building's main entrance is inscribed, "Defend the Children of the Poor & Punish the Wrongdoer." The statute of Lady Justice on the dome is thought to show Blind Justice, but the blindfold is missing! *Courtesy of D. Peter Lund*

Although many pirate stories talk about buried treasure, findings of such treasure are rare according to researchers. The treasure more often ended up at the bottom of the sea or in the pockets of the shop owners in the pirate's favorite ports, such as Port Royal, Jamaica, where they squandered their booty on demon rum, buxom beauties, and 24-hour gambling.

One such captain was John Kidd during the late 1600s or the "Golden Age of Piracy." A Scotsman, John Kidd resided in New York. He was trained as a sailor and called the "Wizard of the Seas." Because he owned a small boat, he knew many pirates and their haunts. When he was with the pirates, he talked and acted as they did. When he was conversing with law-abiding New York citizens, he would talk about how easy it would to get rid of the pirates and to prevent their harassment of good citizens such as himself.

In 1695, King William III appointed the Earl of Bellamont to govern New England and New York. A good administrator, he heard many complaints about the piracies committed in the West Indies and along the eastern seaboard. The Earl of Bellamont decided to put an end to the pirates. At the bequest of several concerned gentlemen, he commissioned John Kidd, who talked as if he knew a good deal about pirates, to take and seize the pirates and bring them to justice. Accordingly, the government purchased and manned a vessel called the *Adventure Galley* and appointed John Kidd Captain.

On a beautiful sunny morning, Captain Kidd and his crew went off to find the pirates. But instead of catching pirates, they themselves became the pirates, taking and selling ships and disposing of the cargoes. Ultimately, Kidd was captured and sent to England because he was a notorious pirate. The

Until 1783, public executions took place at Tyburn, which is near today's Marble Arch. After the execution, surgeons' assistants and friends of the victim often struggled for possession of the corpse. The former wanted it for teaching anatomy, and the latter wanted to give it a proper burial. After 1783, public executions were carried out in this square. *Courtesy of D. Peter Lund*

wretched malefactor was tried at Old Bailey and sentenced to be hung. When he fell to the ground, he was hung again, once he had professed his charity to the assembled crowd and his hopes for salvation.

# Rahere's Sandals and Other Ghostly Appearances

*London churches have seen a great deal of history. Of course, ghosts are strongly associated with religion because many people associate ghosts with the dead or life after death.*

Henry I, the fourth son of William the Conqueror, succeeded his brother William II as King of England in 1100. One of his favorite courtiers was the multi-talented Rahere. In addition to being a courtier, he was a clerk, jester, and clergyman.

In 1120, Henry I controlled a large empire that spread from England to Normandy. Merchants and courtiers sailed the English Channel in longboats, the medieval equivalent of a ferry. A young sea captain approached Henry as he was preparing to sail from Barfleur, France, to England; he suggested that Henry sail on his new state-of-the-art longboat, the *White Ship*. Henry decided he would allow his son and heir William to sail on this longboat with many other young nobles, the cream of the Norman society at that time. Like all fathers, he wanted to give his son a special treat. When the *White Ship* set out, its passengers broke out the wine and held a great party. As the party became more raucous, they dared the captain, who had also been indulging in wine, to overtake the King's ship, which was ahead of them. The fifty oarsmen rowed strongly, but the ship hit a rock, which shattered the hull. The beautiful new ship capsized almost immediately. The King's son and almost everyone else aboard perished.

When Henry's only legitimate male heir, along with the sons and daughters of many courtiers, drowned with

A Scottish hero, Sir William Wallace was a Scottish knight, landowner, and patriot who defied the English and united the clans during the Scottish Wars of Independence. *Courtesy of D. Peter Lund*

the sinking of the *White Ship*, his court became quite dismal. As this was certainly not a good environment for a jester, Rahere turned to the church and took a pilgrimage to Rome.

On his way, Rahere became ill with malarial fever. According to the legend, St. Bartholomew appeared to him in a vision, saying that a hospital, as well as a priory church, should be built in his name. In turn, he promised Rahere that prayers for healing made in his church would always be heard and answered.

Feeling much improved physically and knowing that he had a saint watching out for him, Rahere felt that life was once again good. He returned to London where Henry I granted him permission to build a hospital and a church on the large and flat fields at Smithfield.

The priory church, the second oldest in London, and the hospital were often sites for major events in London's history. Following his trial in 1305, William Wallace was taken from

Westminister, stripped naked, and dragged through the city at the heels of a horse to Smithfield, where he was hanged, drawn, and quartered. A plaque in a wall of St. Bartholomew's Hospital near the site of Wallace's execution at Smithfield commemorates this event. To this day, many visit the site of the man known as "Braveheart" and leave flowers in his memory.

At Smithfield in 1381, in front of twenty thousand people, Wat Tyler, a leader of the Peasants' Revolt, came to negotiate with fifteen-year-old King Richard II. Instead, however, the Lord Mayor of London slashed the unarmed Wat Tyler to the ground and the King told the rebels to return home, promising them charters of freedom. Later, the King broke this promise of freedom and had the rebel leaders killed. Later, Smithfield became well known for the Marian persecutions (see "Burn Baby Burn").

Let us return, however, to St. Bart's in the days of Rahere.

### The Ghost of St. Bartholomew the Great

Even on a bright spring day, St. Bart's feels old. Inscriptions on the tombs are eroded by weather, the Norman interior has massive stone pillars and elegant arches that have figured in many movies, and the dust moves slowly in the light. St. Bartholomew's is the second oldest church in London—the Norman Chapel of St. John in the Keep of the Tower of London is the oldest.

Rahere was in charge of the hospital until 1137, when he retired to the priory. He became the first prior of the Church of St. Bartholomew the Great. He died in 1144 and is entombed there.

Until the church building was restored, ghosts had never walked inside. Nothing had happened to give creaky life to the old stone floors or to emit cold drafts from somewhere above. But during a nineteenth century restoration, a curious

Rahere, a jester-turned-monk, is said to walk St. Bartholomew the Great, the church he founded. *Courtesy of D. Peter Lund*

soul opened Rahere's sarcophagus; that was not a good move. Not content with looking at the prior's skeleton, the same person is said to have stolen one of Rahere's sandals. Ever since, Rahere has been heard wandering around the church searching for his sandal. Some people have reported seeing the figure of a monk wandering through the church.

Another story relates that thieves broke into the tomb of a prior or knight and scattered his bones and other articles about the church. Eventually, everything was returned except a single shinbone. Perhaps the noise is the missing shinbone shuffling through the church!

### St. Bartholomew's Hospital

In medieval times, members of monastic orders played major roles alleviating sickness and suffering. In

England alone, there were approximately seven hundred and fifty religious houses. St. Bartholomew's Hospital, which still exists, was founded as a sanctuary for the ill, the aged and the homeless. From the day it was built, the hospital radiated healing power. True believers felt that the blind could see again, the deaf could hear again, and cripples could walk away healed.

In 1546, King Henry VIII granted St. Bart's hospital to the City of London. At that time, the statue of the king was installed above the main gates. *Courtesy of D. Peter Lund*

Medieval hospital patients were provided with comfort and bland diets, and monks or nuns were attentive to their physical and spiritual needs. Even after the sick were healed of their infirmity, they were not sent home directly, but were kept for several more days to guard against relapses.

The hospital has its own ghosts. A nurse who committed suicide after accidentally killing a patient with a morphine overdose is known as the Grey Lady of Grace Ward. Nurses have felt her tapping their shoulder and shaking her head in warning. In mornings after a ghostly occurrence, the sun lights up dust motes in the place where she had been standing.

A haunted elevator takes passengers down to the basement whether they request it or not. Storytellers say that a nurse was murdered in the elevator and her spirit causes the elevator to head for the basement where the morgue is. Perhaps she is lonely.

When Henry VIII dissolved the monasteries, the hospital lost its only source of income, but the king finally agreed to reestablish the hospital in 1546. A statue of King Henry is above the hospital gate, which was built in 1702. When the National Health Service was founded in 1948, it officially became known as St. Bartholomew's Hospital.

Today, the hospital is the oldest surviving hospital in London and has a great museum attached to it. Filled with interesting artifacts and medical instruments, the museum provides a remarkable insight to the development of medical knowledge and treatment of the sick over the ages.

**Author's Note:** St. Bartholomew the Great church survived the Great Fire of 1666, the Zeppelin raids of World War I, and the Blitz of World War II. Today, it is an active Anglican/ Episcopal Church, with a reputation not only for wonderful architecture but also for traditional formal worship, marvelous music, and intelligent preaching. It has appeared in a series of award-winning films, including *Four Weddings and a Funeral, Shakespeare in Love, The End of the Affair, Amazing Grace,* and *Elizabeth: The Golden Age.*

**Directions:** Exit the St. Paul Underground Station, proceed up Aldersgate Street, and make a left on Cloth Fair.

# The Portrait

Hanging calmly in London's National Portrait Gallery is the portrait of a strikingly handsome, seventeeth-century gentleman. His long dark hair curls around his face, his eyes are dark, and his lips curl. This portrait of the Duke of Monmouth was painted after the man was dead, from five chops of the executioner's axe!

According to legend, an astute civil servant realized that no portrait had ever been painted of the duke, just as his head and body were about to be buried. What a dilemma; he was the son of a King, after all! So the head was stitched back onto the body, the corpse was dressed in royal attire, and it sat for its portrait to be painted.

But we must begin at the beginning. James Scott, Duke of Monmouth, was the first (there were several) illegitimate son of King Charles II of England. His mother was Lucy Walter, a pretty Welsh girl who was the first of at least fifteen mistresses. Charles met Lucy in The Hague in the summer of 1648; Lucy gave birth to James in 1649. Unfortunately, she didn't remain faithful to Charles, so he left her.

Young James was brought to England in 1663, several years after his father was restored to the monarchy. At the age of 14, he became Duke of Monmouth, Earl of Doncaster, and Baron Scott of Tynedale. He and the wealthy Scottish heiress, Anne Scott, fourth Countess of Buccleuch, were married and named the Duke and Duchess of Buccleuch.

Young Monmouth had inherited his father's physique and his mother's beauty, and he resembled a Stuart. His father adored him. But that wasn't sufficient for the Duke of Monmouth. He longed for more. He wanted the crown of England.

Most of us know that we can't always have what we want, but there are those who just don't get that fact through their heads. Monmouth dearly wanted to be Charles' heir. He said to himself, "I am the Duke of Monmouth. I am Protestant and able to assume the royal arms with the bar sinister. Charles' Queen appears to be barren, and I am his first born. Why can't I be his heir?"

Since the reign of Bloody Mary, the English had sworn that they would not have a Catholic monarch on the throne. James, Charles' younger brother and the Duke of York, was the heir presumptive to the throne, if the Queen did not bear King Charles a legitimate heir. James, Monmouth's uncle, had leanings towards Roman Catholicism, which was unacceptable to many after the fires of Smithfield. Monmouth asked himself, "Is the nation prepared to accept a Catholic King or will it demand the popular Protestant son of Charles II?" Certainly, he knew the answer; he just needed to convince everyone else.

Monmouth looked after his appearance, spent time with fortunetellers and ignored his wife. (He didn't ignore her totally; they had seven children!) He preened and posed, complained and whined. Meanwhile, he dreamed and told many that the heir should not be James, Duke of York, but James, Duke of Monmouth.

In 1665, at the age of 16, Monmouth served in the English fleet under his uncle, the Duke of York, in the Second Anglo-Dutch War. Later in the war, he returned to England to assume his first military command of a troop of cavalry. At the age of 21, he became the senior army officer when the Captain General of the army died in 1670. Monmouth's popularity increased, and he was considered one of Britain's finest soldiers.

In 1678 Monmouth commanded a brigade, fighting for the United Provinces (i.e., the Netherlands) against the French. He distinguished himself at the battle of St. Denis, further enhancing his reputation. The following year, after his return to Britain, he commanded the small army, which defeated the rebellion of the Scottish Covenanters (i.e., hard-core Presbyterians). By this time it was becoming apparent that Charles II and his Queen would have no legitimate heir, and the Protestant Monmouth was regarded by many as preferable to the Catholic Duke of York.

Monmouth continued to have grandiose dreams of being the King of England. He became involved in the unsuccessful Rye House Plot of 1683, a plan to assassinate his uncle and father. Monmouth went into exile in Holland. When Charles II died, he led the "Monmouth Rebellion," an attempt to take the throne from his uncle. He declared himself King and was crowned in several towns.

When the soldiers of King James II defeated his forces at the battle of Sedgemoor on 6 July 1685, Monmouth was captured and arrested. Parliament declared him guilty without a trial, and he was executed on July 15, 1685, on Tower Hill. Supposedly, the executioner, the famous Jack Ketch, took at least five strokes with his axe and finally used a knife to sever Monmouth's head from his shoulders.

*And that was when the Duke of Monmouth sat for his official portrait.*

*Incidentally, Monmouth was right about one thing. England would not stand for a Catholic King for long. James II was eventually dethroned in 1688 in the course of the Glorious Revolution. He was the last Catholic monarch to rule Britain.*

**Directions:** National Portrait Gallery is in Trafalgar Square. The nearest Tube is Leicester Square or Charing Cross.

On 16 October 1834, fire destroyed most of Westminister Palace. It was rebuilt, but during the Second World War, bombs hit it fourteen times. *Courtesy of Thomas P. Rooney*

# A Cloistered Existence

Royalty is not always a happy state of being. One of the royal residences that has had its share of sad princesses is Kensington Palace, which was once the home of Diana, Princess of Wales. Centuries before, another unhappy royal princess dwelled there.

George III and his wife Charlotte had thirteen children who survived to adulthood. Their family was not a happy one. King George, who was considered mad (he had porphyria, a metabolic disease), endured many painful remedies such as having leeches applied to his forehead and his scalp blistered in efforts to draw the poisonous matter from his brain. Frequently confined in a straitjacket with his arms tied around his back, he was given strong purges and left in icy cold rooms. His sons had reputations for enjoying women, drinking, gambling and running up huge debts – none of which makes a father happy.

Unable to manage his infamous sons, George III decided that he would control his daughters. Rather than using them as diplomatic pawns, he and his wife shut the six princesses (Charlotte, Augusta, Elizabeth, Mary, Sophia and Amelia) away from the world. Instead of training them to be Queens, they wanted them to become obedient royal companions for their parents. The princesses were not allowed to mix with anyone outside the Royal Court. They weren't allowed to read anything that hadn't been approved, were rarely without a chaperone, and had every hour of their day planned for them.

With access only to their father, brothers and, occasionally, household staff, the girls knew little about men. One of their parents' goals was to keep them chaste! Although they were better educated than was usual for young women of that era, they were not allowed to marry until they were past their childbearing years. The princesses referred to their cloistered existence as "the nunnery."

The fifth daughter Sophia was considered the most intelligent and one of the most attractive. Sophia and her sisters often visited Weymouth, a coastal town in southern England, for resting and cures. One of George III's equerries, General Thomas Garth, leased a house not far from Weymouth so to be accessible to the King during his visits. Unfortunately for everyone involved, Sophia and her sisters visited this house on their journeys to Weymouth. While there, Sophia seemed to have had sufficient time alone with the fifty-six-year-old General Garth to have embarked on an affair.

In August 1800, the twenty-two year-old Sophia gave birth to a boy she named Thomas, undoubtedly after his father. Apparently, the entire family – except for the king – knew of Sophia's pregnancy and the subsequent birth of her son. To explain Sophia's increasing girth and absence, the King was told that she had dropsy, which caused her to be bloated and that she had to be sent away to recover. When she returned to court, he was told that roast beef cured her. Amazingly or perhaps in a muddled moment, the King accepted the story of the miraculous roast beef cure.

Baby Thomas was left at the Weymouth home of the King's private secretary, and later General Garth adopted him. Although the palace never officially recognized the existence of Thomas, the unofficial stance was that General Garth was indeed the natural father, which the court generally accepted.

Some, however, believed a nasty rumor concerning Sophia's alleged incestuous relationship with her brother, Ernest Augustus, Duke of Cumberland (see "The Headless Valet"). The rumor went so far as to pinpoint him as the "real" father of the child.

Garth managed to retain his position at court and was even appointed to the household of Princess Charlotte. Poor Sophia,

Kensington Palace was the favorite residence of successive sovereigns until 1760 and the birthplace of Queen Victoria. Today, Kensington Palace accommodates the offices and private apartments of a number of members of the Royal Family and several ghosts. *Courtesy of D. Peter Lund*

without son or lover, was condemned to a lonely spinster existence in her Kensington Palace apartments. As time passed, her eyesight began to fail. Eventually, she became a sad, pathetic figure whose only solace was to sit at her spinning wheel. Perhaps like the princess in the Rumplestilskin story, she relived her dreams to the tune of that creaking rhythmic spinning wheel. Tragically, even this diversion became impossible when she could no longer see at all. She was moved to nearby York House, where she lived out the remainder of her days.

Her spirit, however, often returns to the rooms at Kensington Palace where she suffered so much unhappiness. Today, when a whirring noise is heard in the palace, one wonders if it is just the wind or is it Sophie at her spinning wheel?

**Directions:** Exit High Street Kensington station through the shopping center and turn right on Kensington High Street. Cross the road opposite the Royal Garden Hotel and enter Kensington Gardens. The Palace is signposted, but basically it's straight ahead.

# "Vy Dondt Dey Com"

Kensington Palace in London remains an official royal residence, although a reigning monarch no longer uses it.

In 1689 , King William III , an asthmatic, bought the early seventeenth century mansion called Nottingham House from the Earl of Nottingham, his Secretary of State, because he wanted a residence away from the sooty London environment. Christopher Wren constructed Royal Apartments for the King and Queen, a council chamber, the Chapel Royal, and the Great Stairs. A private road, wide enough for three or four carriages to travel abreast, was laid out from the palace to Hyde Park Corner

George II spent his last days at Kensington Palace anxiously awaiting the arrival of long overdue dispatches from his beloved Hanover, Germany. Legend tells us that he would glance up at the weather vane that stood over the entrance, watching for the wind to change direction and speed his messengers to him. His courtiers would hear him muttering in broken English, "Vy dondt dey com?" When the dispatches finally did arrive, he had already died.

Many say they have seen his wraith-like face at the window of his chambers, staring at the palace weather vane. Others have reported hearing a voice saying, "Vy dondt dey com?"

All important prisoners entered the Tower through the water gate under St. Thomas's Tower known as Traitors Gate. According to legend, when Mary I sent her sister Elizabeth to the Tower, the latter angrily declared that she was not a traitor and would not pass through the gate. Later, when she was Queen Elizabeth, she insisted on passing through Traitors Gate. "What was good enough for Elizabeth the Princess is good enough for Elizabeth the Queen," she is said to have told the Constable. *Courtesy of D. Peter Lund*

# Bibliography


Aberth, John. *From the Brink of the Apocalypse.* New York: Routledge, 2003.

Abbott, Geoffrey. *Execution.* New York: St. Martin's Press, 2005.

Brigden, Susan. *New Worlds, Lost Worlds: The Rule of The Tudors*. New York: Viking, 2001.

Byrne, Joseph Patrick. *Daily Life during the Black Death*. Westport, Connecticut: Greenwood Press, 2006.

Chrimes, S. B. *Lancastrians, Yorkists, and Henry V*. London: MacMillan & Co Ltd., 1964.

Clive, Mary. *This Sun of York. New* York: Alfred Knopf. 1974.

Coote, Stephen. *Royal Survivor*. New York: St. Martin's Press, 1999.

Cummins, John G. *Francis Drake*. New York: St. Martin's Press, 1995.

Defoe, Daniel. *A Journal of the Plague Year*. New York: Penguin Classics, 2003.

Ditmas, E. M. R. "The Way Legends Grow." *Folklore*. Vol 85 (4) p. 244-265, Winter, 1974.

Doherty, Paul. *Isabella and the Strange Death of Edward I.* New York: Carroll & Graf Publishers, 2003.

Felber, Edith. *Queen of Shadows.* New York: New American Library, 2006.

Foxe, John. *Book Of Martyrs.* Boston: Little, Brown, 1966.

Gibson, Michael. *Charles II*. East Sussex, England: Wayland Publishers, 1976.

Hyamson, Albert M. *History of the Jews in England.* Honolulu, Hawaii, University Press of Pacific. 2001.

Jones, Richard. *Walking Haunted London.* Northhampton, Massachusetts: Interlink Books: 2007.

Knapp, Andrew. *The Newgate Calendar.* New York: Capricorn Books, 1962.

Lace, William W. *The Little Princes in the Tower.* San Diego, California: Lucent Books. 1997.

Lacey, Robert. *Great Tales from English History.* New York: Back Bay Books, 2007.

Meyer, Carolyn. *Mary, Bloody Mary.* New York: Scholastic, Inc., 2000.

Newman, Paul B. *Growing up in the Middle Ages*. Jefferson, North Carolina: McFarland & Company, 2007.

Parkes, James William. *The Jew in the Medieval Community.* New York: Hermon Press, 1976.

Pierce, Hael. *Margaret Pole, Countess of Salisbury*. Cadiff: University of Wales: 2003.

Prestwich, Michael. *The Three Edwards : War and State.* London: Routledge. 1990.

Raban, Sandra. *England under Edward I and Edward II 1259-1327.* Cornwall: Blackwell Publishers, 2000.

Slavicek, Louise Chipley. *Bloody Mary.* Detroit: Thomson & Gale. 2005.

Talbot, C. H. *Medicine in Medieval England.* New York: American Elsevier Publishing Company, Inc., 1967.

Warnicke, Retha M. *The Rise And Fall of Anne Boleyn.* Cambridge, 1989.

Wedgwood, C. V. *A Coffin for King Charles*. New York: The MacMillan Company, 1964.

Weir, Alison, *The Princes in the Tower.* New York: Ballantine Books. 1992.

______. *Queen Isabella.* New York: Ballantine Books. 2005.

# Index